# THIS MIGHTY DREAM

SOCIAL PROTEST MOVEMENTS IN THE UNITED STATES

Madeleine Adamson and Seth Borgos

DESIGNED BY JOHN BEAM

Routledge & Kegan Paul

BOSTON, LONDON, MELBOURNE AND HENLEY

*First published in 1984*
*by Routledge & Kegan Paul plc*

*9 Park Street, Boston, Mass. 02108, USA,*
*14 Leicester Square, London WC2H 7PH,*
*464 St Kilda Road, Melbourne, Victoria 3004, Australia,*
*and*
*Broadway House, Newton Road, Henley-on-Thames, Oxon*
*RG9 1 EN*

*Set in English Times, 9½ on 11½ pt.*
*by Meisel Media, Baltimore*
*Printed in the United States of America*

*Publication of this book has been aided by a grant from the*
*National Endowment for the Humanities.*

**Library of Congress Cataloging in Publication Data**
Adamson, Madeleine, 1951-
  This mighty dream.

Bibliography: p.
1. Radicalism—United States. 2. United States—Social conditions.
3. Social movements—United States.
I. Borgos, Seth, 1952-  .        II. Title.
HN90.R3A3 1984     322.4'4'0973     84-16111
ISBN 0-7102-0040-4
ISBN 0-7102-0042-0 (pbk.)

*Grateful acknowledgement is made for permission to reprint*
*the following previously published material.*

*Excerpts of the Langston Hughes poem, "Let America Be*
*America." Reprinted by permission of Harold Ober As-*
*sociates Incorporated. Copyright 1938 by Langston Hughes.*
*Copyright renewed 1965 by Langston Hughes.*

*Quotations by Bayard Rustin, John Lewis, James Farmer,*
*Ed Gardner, Amzie Moore, Lawrence Guyot, Dave Dennis,*
*and Charles Cobb. Reprinted by permission of the Putnam*
*Publishing Group from* My Soul is Rested *by Howell Raines.*
*Copyright 1977 by Howell Raines.*

*Quotations by H.L. Mitchell, George Stith, Carrie*
*Dillworth, Clay East, and J.R. Butler. Reprinted by permis-*
*sion of Southern Exposure from* Working Lives: The Southern Exposure History of Labor in the South. *Copyright 1974*
*by the Institute for Southern Studies.*

# Contents

I am the poor white, fooled and pushed apart,
I am the Negro bearing slavery's scars.
I am the red man driven from the land,
I am the immigrant clutching the hope I seek—
And finding only the same old stupid plan
Of dog eat dog, of mighty crush the weak.

O, let America be America again—
The land that never has been yet—
And yet must be—
The land where *every* man is free.
The land that's mine—
The poor man's, Indian's, Negro's, ME—
Who made America,
Whose sweat and blood, whose faith and pain,
Whose hand at the foundry, whose plow in the rain,
Must bring back our mighty dream again.

O, yes,
I say it plain,
American never was America to me,
And yet I swear this oath—
America will be!

Langston Hughes

To the members of ACORN, who sustain the dream.

# Preface

*This Mighty Dream* evolved from a traveling exhibit and interpretive program sponsored by ACORN, a national community organization with a membership of 50,000 low and moderate income families. When Routledge & Kegan Paul invited the authors to prepare a pictorial volume based on the exhibit, it seemed at once a fitting conclusion to this alternately vexing and inspiring project and a good means to expose it to a wider audience.

As ACORN staff members, years before the project's genesis, we were mindful of the organization's roots in the rich and varied tradition of American protest. Chief organizer Wade Rathke, in a staff training manual, acknowledged a string of historical debts: "ACORN drew on the unique experience of the Southern Tenant Farmers Union, established a membership dues system similar to the unions, and defined its efforts statewide like welfare rights organizations. This statewide organization consisted of local neighborhood-based groups in the Alinsky tradition, planned for alternative service centers like the Community Service Organization, and depended on large numbers of skilled organizers as did the Nonpartisan League."

But by 1980, after a decade of rapid growth, few of ACORN's members were conversant with this background, even though many of them, or their parents and grandparents, had been active with the organization's predecessors. And the allies, politicians, students, and neighbors ACORN leaders encountered were even less familiar with this history. Having attained national scope and stature, and a certain amount of organizational maturity, it seemed an appropriate time to place ACORN's day-to-day strivings—its protests, pot-lucks, and press releases—into a broader context of social struggle. From this notion came the concept of an educational program on American protest movements.

With Charles Koppelman of the Institute for Social Justice, a training center affiliated with ACORN, we fashioned a submission to the National Endowment for the Humanities. It proposed, in addition to a traveling exhibit, a set of radio documentaries, an array of printed materials, and a series of local events. Their purpose was to encourage ACORN members and the general public to examine present-day goals, values, and strategies for social change in the light of a century's history of protest.

James Early at the Endowment recognized ACORN's capacity to reach an audience for the humanities which was unconventional by the agency's standards. He shepherded the proposal through the grants award process and remained a staunch, if critical, advocate through ensuing controversies.

Bart Laws joined us from his post as a Philadelphia organizer and took on a lion's share of the work to bring the project to life. He haunted far-flung archives and libraries to uncover a wealth of materials, including the

Langston Hughes poem that gave this book its name.

In the project planning stages, we drew on the advice and assistance of an able corps of academics and activists, including Richard Cloward, Gary Delgado, Lawrence Goodywn, Marilyn Gittell, Jose Angel Gutierrez, Warren Haggstrom, Hulbert James, George Lipsitz, Frances Fox Piven, George Rawick, Bernice Johnson Reagon, and Lee Staples. Other scholars contributed detailed synopses of individual movements and identified sources of photographs and illustrations: Russell Adams on the Populists and the black freedom movement, Eileen Boris on the role of women in social protest, Esther Bromberg on the forerunners of modern community organizing, and Scott Ellsworth on the origins of the Nonpartisan League. Bill Pastreich, Tim Sampson, and Bert DeLeeuw, all welfare rights veterans, mined their personal "archives" and memories for insights and artifacts.

Bert DeLeeuw, who combines carpentry with organizing, also devised a sturdy but portable design for the exhibit and built the 40-odd panels. John Beam, a Baltimore graphic artist, created an effective format to present hundreds of photos, flyers, quotes, and text, and spent countless hours assembling the panels.

Though not quite complete, the exhibit made its debut in St. Louis in early 1982 and arrived in Memphis for the 50th anniversary celebration of the Southern Tenant Farmers Union.

In the midst of frantic preparations for the squatters tent city that summer, we burned the midnight oil to complete the exhibit panels in time for an official opening at ACORN's national convention in Philadelphia. Members from across the country had their first view of "This Mighty Dream" between boisterous marches on the Democratic Party mid-term convention.

Over the next year, Shelly Benkaim and Yvonne Wyborney crisscrossed the U.S. in a bright red step van delivering the exhibit to more than a dozen cities. It was displayed at public libraries, colleges, union and church halls, and even a shopping mall in Sioux Falls, South Dakota. At each location, a series of public events used the exhibit plus films, performances, and panel presentations as springboards for discussion. The sessions frequently highlighted indigenous protest traditions; in Sioux Falls, one program examined the historic parallels between a 1938 strike at a local meat packing plant and a contemporary strike against the same firm. A forum in St. Paul traced the evolution of direct action tactics in the labor movement, civil rights struggles, and community organizing, and probed the ethics of civil disobedience.

While the exhibit toured the country, Cliff Kuhn produced four radio documentaries jointly titled, "Democratic Moments." Gwen Cyrkiel, Karen Miller, and Bill Pease published special editions of the membership newspaper, *USA*, and Bill pinch-hit for us in numerous crises.

The unfailing help of D.C. staffers Larry Ginsburg, Susan Bissenden, and Carolyn Carr—on everything from painting panels to project paperwork—kept things running smoothly. And the entire project benefited from the advice of two skilled evaluators, Peter Wood and Will Collette.

By 1983, one element of the program remained unfinished—a guidebook to accompany the exhibit. At Bill Ryan's suggestion, Carol Baker of Routledge & Kegan Paul paid us a visit, and she persuaded us to revise our modest plans and produce this volume. In the year from conception to completion, Carol offered lavish encouragement, and Stratford Caldecott stepped in after her departure to oversee the final stages.

In the transition from exhibit to book, many archivists, librarians, and curators aided our research. We owe special thanks to Jennifer Bright at the Museum of the City of New York, D. Louise Cook at the Martin Luther King, Jr. Center for Nonviolent Social Change, Edith Mayo at the Smithsonian Institution Museum of American History, Harold Miller at the State Historical Society of Wisconsin, Walter Naegle at the A. Philip Randolph Educational Fund, Larry Remele at the State Historical Society of North Dakota, and Jane Stevens at the Chicago Historical Society. "Movement" photographers Bob Fitch, Roland Freeman, Robert Gumpert, Doug Harris, and Matt Herron responded generously to our requests. And it was a special pleasure to consult with H.L. Mitchell, founder of the Southern Tenant Farmers Union, and Fred Ross, the principal organizer of CSO.

Richard Kazis and Steve Kest offered helpful criticisms on the labor history portion of the manuscript. Margie Snider and Gwen Cyrkiel did the taxing work of proofreading. Bart Laws was always on call with a remarkable ability to recollect obscure facts and photo sources.

Now would be the appropriate time to thank a crew of typists or perhaps expound on the merits of word processing machines, but we produced this book the old fashioned way, perfecting our typing skills on many drafts.

This was a collaborative effort in every other respect and we are grateful to the scores of people whose contributions made it possible, especially to Bart Laws for laying the groundwork, and to Gwen Cyrkiel and John Beam for their unstinting personal support. Above all, we are indebted to the leaders and organizers of ACORN with whom we have shared a mighty dream and struggled to make it real.

# Foreword

by  Frances Fox Piven  and
Richard A. Cloward

This book is a record of some of the great popular protest movements of American history. But it appears at a time when activists seem to have turned away from movements in favor of electoral politics, although for diverse reasons and with diverse strategies. Some, jarred by the election of 1980 and the dramatic changes in national policy that followed, have moved into the Democratic Party fold, in effect promising allegiance to anyone but Reagan in 1984. Others have been more assertive, attempting to enlarge the possibilities of electoral politics by enlisting under Jesse Jackson's banner, or, as feminists have done, by acting as a pressure group demanding concessions from within the Democratic Party. Still others have joined in voter registration campaigns, some simply hoping to defeat Reagan, others more ambitiously hoping both to beat Reagan and to transform the Democratic Party by enlarging its constituency to include substantially more of the poor and minorities.

One way to interpret the renewed emphasis on electoral politics is that it reflects a certain disillusionment on the Left with the movement politics of the 1960s and early 1970s. This interpretation seems credible because movement and electoral strategies have come to be seen as polarized alternatives. Those who reject electoral politics do so on the grounds that movement constituencies and the issues they raise would inevitably be swallowed up in the electoral morass, exhausting their energies in exchange for token responses. In turn, that view receives support and standing from a good deal of the work of the intellectual Left which defines electoral politics, in a nutshell, as a system of ritual legitimation of prevailing structures of power and inequality. Viewed from this perspective, those on the Left who choose electoral politics over movement participation are often judged as having failed a test of conviction.

There is much about this argument that is true. The turn to electoral politics does usually result in the absorption of movement leaders and the dissipation of movement energies with little recompense in policy concessions. The reasons are obvious. On the one side, movement leaders rarely represent blocs of votes sufficiently large to command concessions. And even when the adherents are numerous, movement leaders do not have the resources to organize and hold their votes against the onslaught of propaganda and promises of party leaders.

On the other side, movement leaders striving for electoral influence must contend with the enormous countervailing power of business. By their capacity to marshall and comunicate "expert" opinion, business leaders ordinarily dominate debates over definitions and solutions to economic crises. They also wield the powerful weapons of capital strike and capital flight, which can destabilize an economy. Few political leaders feel secure enough to weather the economic instabilities that these investor tactics create, or to invoke sanctions to prevent their use, as the experience of the Italian Communists and the French Socialists reveal. Moreover, the influence of business on the political parties by conventional means is also growing. The state and local infrastructure of the old party organizations has been virtually superceded by big money propaganda operations, including the rapidly swelling contributions funnelled directly to candidates through Political Action Committees. Against these formidable resources, voters have only their votes with which to contend for influence in party circles.

All of this notwithstanding, the relationship of movements to electoral politics is not one of simple antithesis. In a large and important sense, electoral strategies from the bottom depend on movement politics. Advocates of the electoral path to reform typically assume that votes are automatically translated into influence, or that at least organized votes are automatically translated into influence. The accounts that follow in this volume of the way the electoral effects of the Populists and the North Dakota Nonpartisan League were first twisted and then aborted by the influence of money reveals the fraility of that assumption. Nevertheless, there are conditions under which voters do matter, under which voters can force responses, and those conditions depend critically on the emergence of movements.

Voters become more important to politicians, and have some influence on the agenda of electoral politics, when their allegiance cannot be taken for granted. Large-scale events like war or rapid economic change may generate the discontents which loosen established party allegiances. When electoral volatility increases, political leaders try to protect or rebuild their coalitions by searching for the symbols, promises, and policy concessions that will hold old voters or win new voters, without at the same time provoking opposition elsewhere among their constituent groups.

At such moments of electoral instability, mass protest movements can play a catalytic role, as the movements of industrial workers and the unemployed did in the '30s or the civil rights and anti-war movements in the '60s. Movements sometimes generate such disruptive effects as to break the grip of ruling groups, so that new definitions and new policies can be advanced from the bottom. The issues generated by masses of defiant people politicize and activate voters; they widen divisions in the electorate; and they sometimes attract new voters to the polls who alter the electoral calculus. When political leaders make policy concessions, it is to cope with these threats of electoral cleavage, or to rebuild coalitions in the aftermath of cleavage. The impact of disruptive mass movements on public policy is thus mediated by the electoral system. Movements win policy concessions when the issues they raise fragment, or threaten to fragment, party coalitions.

If protest movements can thus activate electoral constituencies, and give them political weight, movements in turn depend both for survival and success on the electoral context. For movements to emerge and to grow, their potential followers need to feel some measure of hope, on the one hand, and some sense of safety from severe repression, on the other. Political leaders play a large role in signalling these possibilities. If they risk few repercussions at the polls, they are unlikely to generate the symbolic appeasements which may give movements a sense of strength and courage. They are far more likely to repress the movement at the outset. The risk of repression is even greater when the social base from which movements draw support is substantially underrepresented in the electorate. That is a powerful reason for attempting to ensure that people at the bottom have as large a presence as possible in the electoral system.

Nor are protest movements likely to succeed in pressing new issues onto the political agenda, or to win concessions on these issues, if they cannot mobilize a following among electoral constituencies upon whom political leaders depend. The point is not that policy decisions are in fact simply a reflection of voter preferences rather than economic power. Rather it is that for those who have little economic power, or whose economic power can only be mobilized under extraordinary conditions, votes do provide some protection, and sometimes, in the context of electoral instability and movement mobilization, they even provide some influence.

Taken together, these points of interrelationship reveal the interdependence of disruptive mass movements and electoral institutions. Voter influence is not likely to be realized without the instigating force of protest, and protest movements in turn depend upon the relative size of the electoral constituencies that polarize in their support.

This is not an argument in support of conventional electoral politics. We would be the last to argue that movements should devote their resources to drafting legislative proposals, attending high level conferences, or testifying, or lobbying. Movements do not influence electoral politics by the usual means. Still, the electoral context cannot be ignored, and the most crucial feature of that context is the extent to which the movement's social base is included so that, once activated, politicians are forced to contend for its support on more than symbolic terms.

This brings us to what is indisputably the most important feature of American politics: the low level of electoral participation by the bottom half of the population. The United States has the lowest level of voter participation among the western democracies. Seventy-five to 90 percent of Canadians and Europeans turn out in national elections. Little more than half of the eligible American electorate voted in 1980. The significance of low voting participation for popular protest movements is that the missing half is concentrated among the people who are in effect their potential source of electoral support.

Although experts offer differing explanations of the persisting low registration rate, there is a growing consensus that the main causes are difficulties associated with the distinctive American system of voter registration. Other Western democracies have some form of universal registration, and the United States does not. When turnout among registered voters in the United States is compared with turnout in Europe, differences disappear. About 80 percent of Americans who are registered also vote. And they vote in roughly the same proportions no matter their age, education, or minority status. The problem in the United States is that 55 million people—35 percent of the eligible electorate—are not registered. The history of how this came to be is instructive.

Ironically, white working men in the United States won the franchise earlier than workers in other nations. The bulk of the states had removed property qualifications by the early 1830s, at least a half century earlier than most of Europe. At the end of the 19th century, however, as class conflict on the farms and in the factories was coming to a boil, state governments curtailed this basic right by erecting obstacles to voting. The 1890s were the crucial years—a time when railroad and steel workers engaged in violent strikes and family farmers joined in the great protests of the Populist movement. Throughout the South and West, usurious interest rates and exorbitant railroad and granary charges goaded farmers into action. In response to Populist pressure, a number of states passed legislation regulating railroad and granary fees.

But the Supreme Court quickly acted to defend the big interests, reversing hardwon legislative victories, and so the Populists sought redress in national politics. In 1896, they made a serious bid for power by entering into a coalition with the Democratic Party and segments of the industrial working class. The nascent formation was so threatening that the business classes—in their first major effort to dominate electoral politics—mobilized one of the most vitriolic, and expensive, campaigns in American history.

The Populists were crushed, and in the flush of victory industrial and financial interests in the North and planter interests in the South solidified their hold, and erected barriers to voting. They "reformed" state election laws so that another challenge from below could not be mounted. They introduced poll taxes, literacy tests, and grandfather clauses throughout the South. These measures not only made it impossible for blacks to register, but half of whites as well—the same poor whites who had been the foot soldiers of southern Populism. Nor was the backlash confined to the South. Across the North, literacy examinations, residency tests, and various cumbersome procedures were built into the registration process. By the onset of the Great Depression, registration restrictions had reduced voter turnout from 75 percent in national elections in the latter half of the 19th century to little more than 50 percent. Most of the drop occurred among the ranks of blacks, poor farmers, and industrial workers. And so a contraction of the American electorate took place which persists to this day.

To sum up this history in another way, the reason the United States has the lowest level of voting participation among the western democracies is that the right to vote in the United States was sharply curtailed by the laws and procedures surrounding voter registration. In other words, the elemental right to the franchise is still in dispute. And that is a serious problem for popular protest movements. It means they are more vulnerable to repression—what better case in point than the violence done participants in the southern civil rights struggle?—and it means that the demands raised by protest movements lose force because of the weakness of the electoral constituencies to whom they ultimately appeal.

It is for this reason that the turn to electoral politics in the present period is not, in the longer term sense, a shift away from protest politics at all. Most important, there is ample evidence that, despite persisting barriers, large scale voter registration efforts have been spurred by the growing polarization of electoral politics by class, race and gender. The success of these efforts to enlarge the electorate is integral to the future strength of protest movements from the bottom.

*"One cannot demand of whole nations exceptional moral foresight and heroism, but a certain hard common sense in facing the complicated phenomena of political life must be expected in every progressive people. In some respects we as a nation seem to lack this; we have the somewhat inchoate idea that we are not destined to be harassed with great social questions, and that even if we are, and fail to answer them, the fault is with the question and not with us."*

W.E.B. DuBois, 1896

# Introduction

Nearly 90 years after DuBois's observation, Americans seem as reluctant as ever to confront the "great social questions" which underlie our national life. The problem of wealth—*How is it created? What is its function? Who should control it?*—has been reduced to a squabble over the competitive position of American industry. The issue of equity—*How shall the benefits of society be shared?*—is a political stepchild we don't face squarely, though we can't quite banish it from sight. And the central dilemma of democracy—*How shall the people rule?*—is hardly acknowledged, as if it had been solved generations ago.

Yet there have been periods in our history when Americans were compelled to address fundamental questions of national purpose and values. Issues of poverty and equity were thrust onto the evening news in the 1960s; the problem of wealth was a subject of intense popular debate during the Depression; in the years preceding the presidential election of 1896, the entire shape of the American order was questioned. Such moments of collective social criticism have occurred, on a lesser scale, throughout our history, in such unlikely locales as the Wheat Belt counties of North Dakota, the steel towns of the industrial heartland, the hamlets of the Mississippi Delta, and the barrios of California. In some instances they have produced change, in other cases a reinforcement of the existing order. But regardless of outcome, these moments deserve to be celebrated as heroic episodes in our national past.

It is the premise of *This Mighty Dream* that mass-based movements and the conflict they generate are the primary agents of social change in American society. This is hardly the prevailing view. Our national culture, so enamored of individual competition, is wary of social conflict. Americans prefer to think of social change in terms of problems and solutions: the Depression was a problem, the New Deal the solution; discrimination was a problem, the civil rights laws a solution.

But social problems, of themselves, do not generate social change. The elections of the early 1890s became an unofficial referendum on the future course of the nation not because the problems created by the transformation of the U.S. economy were suddenly more urgent, but because a popular insurgency on a national scale forced the question. Racial segregation became a national embarrassment in the 1940s, but it was not dismantled until a mass movement created sufficient political conflict to compel a solution.

Social problems do not delimit the boundaries of change either. The New Deal is less significant for its impact on the Depression, which was marginal, and its humane effects, which were transitory, than for the new popular consensus it embodied—an assumption that government has the obligation to provide a modicum of economic security and the authority to regulate private wealth to that end. This assumption was not always articulated or even shared by the architects of the New Deal. Rather, the history of the 1930s suggests that popular insurgencies—the Unemployed Councils, the Southern Tenant Farmers Union, the industrial union movement—pushed the New Deal forward and interpreted its significance to many Americans. When it coined the famous slogan, "The president wants you to join a union," the CIO exaggerated the intent of Roosevelt's labor policy. Then, as workers responded by the millions to the call, the president was obliged to defend their right to organize.

Similarly, the most far-reaching impact of the black freedom movement was not the dismantling of segregation, but a deepened popular commitment to human equality. Ultimately, if affected not only the standing of blacks but the status and self-image of other political outcasts: Hispanics, Native Americans, women, the handicapped, homosexuals, the old.

When compelled to identify agents of change, Americans tend to select leaders. Thus, Franklin D. Roosevelt becomes a symbol of bold reform, though his instincts and values were essentially conservative, and William Jennings Bryan becomes the embodiment of Populism, though he was a latecomer to the movement and his "silver crusade" was a diversion, if not a betrayal, of the Populist impulse. The role of Martin Luther King, Jr., a genuine protest leader, has been magnified to the point that a young person may be forgiven for assuming that King's magnificent rhetoric single-handedly moved millions to knock down the walls of segregation. Like the Roosevelt myth, and the Bryan myth before it, the King myth is inspirational, but it also pernicious, because it obscures the true and painful dynamic of change.

1

In a democracy such as ours, fundamental changes in national values cannot be imposed by a political elite or by charismatic protest leaders. Leaders articulate a vision of change, social problems create a context for it, politicians channel and harness it, but the catalytic ingredient in social change is mass agitation.

*This Mighty Dream* is a critical interpretation of mass movements for social change in the post-Civil War United States. By necessity, it is a selective account and the bases for selection are worth articulating.

All of the movements depicted in *This Mighty Dream* share two fundamental characteristics. They responded to specific and immediate grievances experienced by masses of people at the bottom of society. And while their goals varied, they uniformly employed collective modes of action.

We begin after the Civil War because it represents a convenient and reasonably accurate dividing line between a distant agrarian age and a recognizably modern industrial era. Organizations like the Farmers Alliance and the Knights of Labor were a reaction to the emerging commercial monopolies, and their scope was commensurate with that of their corporate adversaries. The railroad, the telegraph, and other innovations which facilitated large-scale business enterprises also made it possible for the first time to coordinate grassroots action on a national scale. These giant new movements encountered new strategic dilemmas and organizational tensions which are still bedevilling people's organizations today.

We draw an implicit distinction between grassroots protest movements and left wing political formations, and treat the history of the Left only insofar as it influenced grassroots protest. The movements included here generated new ideas about politics and society—some of them crude and narrow in scope, others broad and sophisticated—but for each of them, ideology was subordinate to the exigencies of struggle. The Left, on the other hand, saw ideology as fundamental, believing that without a consistent analysis of society's ills and a comprehensive program for its transformation, efforts to change society were inherently narrow and opportunistic.

This contrast is reflected in the way organizations defined, recruited and maintained their constituencies. Even the left wing parties whose theories enshrined the "working class" in practice recruited their membership from all economic and occupational strata; ideology was the glue that held their heterogenous ranks together. With the possible exception of the Socialist Party during the early part of this century, the parties were never able to build a mass membership on this basis. Some did not really try, conceiving their role as the development of a "vanguard" whose influence would be felt through the force of conviction rather than numbers.

*This Mighty Dream* concentrates instead on grassroots movements which emerged from specific social classes—farmers, steel workers, blacks, tenants. They recruited on a mass basis within those classes and, as a result, often accomodated a wide range of political values and loyalties. Ideological conformity, even if desired, was impossible to enforce without sacrificing the mass character of the organization. Unity was maintained by focusing on common problems and avoiding or finessing divisive issues. The glue which cemented the ranks of these movements was a commitment to certain programatic goals, and equally important, an engagement in mass action—in boycotts, cooperatives, sit-ins, strikes.

This is not to suggest that Grenbackism, Socialism, Communism, and the New Left did not influence grassroots protest. They did, and their influence is acknowledged in *This Mighty Dream*. But the relationship was far less intimate than the relationship between labor organizations and political parties in Europe, for example, or the relationship between national liberation movements and political ideologies in many Third World nations. In the U.S. the formations of the Left and grassroots protest movements developed along such divergent lines that the conventional practice of fusing them in a single radical tradition distorts as much as it clarifies.

The term "grassroots protest" is itself a subject of confusion because protest in the U.S. has emerged from a variety of sources. The anti-imperialist, conservation, and suffrage movements of the pre-World War I era, like the anti-war, environmental, and feminist movements of recent decades, drew their constituency largely from the professional and business classes. Poor people and their organizations participated in these movements, but not in great force and rarely in leadership roles. The poor were far more committed to vehicles such as the Farmers Alliance, labor unions, and community organizations—efforts that began as "poor people's movements," though they did not always remain so— and it is these organizations that constitute the focus of *This Mighty Dream*.

2

The distinction lies deeper than demographics. The strategy and tactics of a movement reflect its social character. Movements with a prominent elite or middle-class constituency usually enjoy better access to public officials and the press, greater financial and technical resources, higher public legitimacy, and immunity from the more severe forms of repression. As a result, they are often able to achieve their goals without recourse to the disruptive tactics which are characteristic of poor people's movements. The objects of protest are different as well. Historically, the protest of the business and professional classes has been aimed at perceived abuses of wealth and power, the protest of the poor and working class at perceived inequities in their distribution.

The point is not that poor people's protest is inevitably more "radical." Some poor people's organizations have been tactically meek and fervently committed to the existing order, while the student-dominated movements of the 1960s—middle-class to the core—employed highly disruptive tactics and posed deep if somewhat muddled challenges to the nation's values. It is the animating impulse which is fundamentally dissimilar.

3

The middle-class protest tradition, though sometimes clothed in political rhetoric, is actually anti-political; the impulse is to curb abuses of wealth and power by removing policy from the framework of competing interests and delivering it to the purer realm of morality and expertise. Utopian on its face, this anti-political idea has always possessed an extraordinary power in the United States, particularly for the professional classes. Indeed, its cultural authority is so great that poor people's organizations have often worn it as a form of camouflage, casting themselves as disinterested public advocates in a sea of self-interested political players. But all of the movements portrayed in *This Mighty Dream* were, in fact, grounded in self-interest—that of the poor and powerless in improving their position. This interest collided with those embodied in the existing structure of wealth and power, and the struggles which resulted were inescapably political.

Within the boundaries we set, there are an abundance of organizations and movements which have carried the mantle of "this mighty dream." EPIC, "Share the Wealth," and the Farm Holiday Associations merit recognition as agents of social change in the 1930s. There are equally compelling stories to be told of the labor struggle in other industries. We might have considered Native American organizing and La Raza Unida. And we might have described the women's suffrage and feminist movements, for they had affinities with poor people's struggles despite their class composition.

But *This Mighty Dream* is not a comprehensive history. It sketches the evolution of certain organizations and events in some detail to illustrate a general interpretation of mass protest in the United States.

While these sketches are drawn mainly from the work of historians and other scholars, they are colored by the distinctive perspective of grassroots organizers. For many, the organizer's role has romantic connotations, suggesting an idealistic if naive youth, an impetuous Prince Charming who seeks to awaken the oppressed with a pure vision and exhortation. For others it evokes a contradictory image, the Organization Man: patient, methodical, and calculating. But the ideal type is both visionary and technician: the technician molds the vision into concrete and realizable form, the visionary liberates the technician from the tyranny of organizational detail. The true organizer must be an exacting critic not only of the existing order but of efforts to change it.

Organizers bring to the historical study of mass movements an intense curiosity about the mechanics of organizational activity. How were new members recruited? How did the organization raise money to cover its expenses? How did it deliver its message to the general public, and how did it apply pressure on its opponents? How did tactics such as the agricultural strike and the sit-in evolve and how, exactly, were they executed?

The answers to these questions are often obscured by myths, propagated not only by an organization's enemies, as one would expect, but also by its partisans. Organizations are rarely candid about operational matters. Democratic procedures may conceal a functioning autocracy; confrontational rhetoric can mask accommodation with the established order. Even where there is no intent to deceive, the technical aspects of organizational recruitment, finances, communications, and tactics are likely to remain obscure to those who are more interested in the organization's "message" than in the mechanics of its delivery. From the organizer's perspective, however, it is just those aspects which are critical in shaping the character of an organization.

The "why" of action is of equal concern to organizers as the "how." Why were certain issues emphasized at certain times? Why were certain targets chosen? Why did an organization expand to new territory? Why were its opponents conciliatory on some occasions, implacable on others? Developments which on first sight appear spontaneous or inevitable often prove to have been deliberate. The Populist idea did not exactly spread "like wildfire" through the South; the process was more like arson, with organizers dispatched by the Texas farmers to light fires in other Southern states.

4

A strategic orientation illuminates the common heritage of the movements portrayed in *This Mighty Dream*. The "unity of struggle" is a cliche of the American Left, often cited, rarely analyzed. There are examples of cooperation, but historically most grassroots movements have been content to cultivate their own constituencies. What the historical record does suggest, however, is that these diverse movements have faced similar organizing problems, and have sometimes benefited, even directly, from each others' experience. The architect of the Montgomery Bus Boycott was E.D. Nixon, a labor movement veteran. Cesar Chavez's approach to organizing farmworkers was shaped by his experience as a community organizer. A recognition of these historical debts represents a sounder basis than pious sentiment for the kinship of struggle.

One further salient element of the organizer's perspective is an appreciation of the role of conflict, which applies not only to the larger theater of social change but to the internal development of organizations. Moments of conflict often reveal more about an organization than platforms and speeches. While popular history tends either to ignore movements for social change or to idealize them, *This Mighty Dream* does not hesitate to depict internal conflicts, along with prejudices, false starts, and strategic errors.

Highlighting these difficulties may seem unsympathetic, but organizers understand from bitter experience that mass movements do not operate in a weightless environment. They are constrained by the existing structure of power, by the cultural assumptions of the moment, by the human limitations and frailties of their leaders. Movements which are serious about social change strive to break free of these restraints; they never succeed entirely. To acknowledge this is not to diminish their heroic stature but to clarify it.

Indeed, while a refusal to accept the constraints of the present environment is a kind of heroism, ignorance of historical obstacles to change is a path to despair. Without access to a living tradition of mass action, it is easy for those who protest today to repeat mistakes, to feel isolated, to lose perspective, to lose hope. Yet a tradition which has been whitewashed to erase the harsh texture of struggle is of little aid to understanding the conflicts and setbacks of the present. Even its inspirational value is ultimately suspect. Social changes, once achieved, become part of the status quo and seem unremarkable to those who come after. It is the spectacle of change wrested from a stubborn adversary that sustains the spirit.

5

**AGRARIAN PROTEST**

# The Farmers Alliance and the People's Party

In the years following the Civil War, the United States entered a new era—the Industrial Age. Rail transportation and factory production transformed the U.S. from an economy of small farms, small business, and local markets to a national market dominated by large banking, railroad, and manufacturing enterprises.

Farmers felt squeezed from all sides. The economy was booming, but farm prices were low and spiralling downward. Railroad monopolies demanded high fees for shipping commodities, and merchants charged high prices and high interest for seed and equipment.

At the heart of the farmers' discontent was their relationship to the financial system. By the nature of their enterprise, farmers are debtors; they borrow in the spring to buy seed and supplies and expect to retire the debt with the proceeds of the harvest. During the post-Civil War era, however, the federal government followed a deliberate policy of monetary contraction, refusing to expand the supply of money as the population and economy grew. This "sound money" policy, as its proponents called it, was staunchly supported by both the Republican and Democratic parties. It produced high interest rates and a steadily more "expensive" dollar, good for bankers and other creditors, but disastrous for debtors.

In the South, impoverished by the war, the vast majority of farmers operated outside the cash economy under the "crop lien system." Farmers obtained supplies on credit from a "furnishing merchant," often at interest rates of 50 percent or higher. For security, the merchant took a lien on the farmer's crop. As commodity prices collapsed and interest rates soared, more and more farmers were unable to pay off their debts at harvest and lost their freedom to a merchant who told them what they could buy and what they could plant.

In response to these conditions, farmers created a multitude of self-help organizations. The most prominent of these in the 1870s was the National Grange. To free its members from the merchants, the Grange experimented with cooperative stores. These stores were run on a cash basis, though, and few farmers had the cash to participate. Unwilling to consider more radical solutions, the Grange became, in effect, a social and educational network for the more affluent class of farmers.

During the same period, a political movement known as the "Greenbackers" posed a direct challenge to the prevailing financial orthodoxy. The Greenbackers advocated a rapid expansion of the money supply, a policy which would have benefited not only farmers but most workers and business entrepreneurs. The insurgency foundered, however, on the sectional loyalties that dominated the politics of the era. Regardless of the pocketbook appeal of the Greenback doctrine, few Southern voters

"By the time the farmer is ready to sell his crop, he is pretty well buried under a pile of debt. He takes his wheat to market, fully believing that it is 'number one hard' but the elevator man's eagle eye promptly discovers that it is 'frosted' or 'damp' and . . . he is forced to sell for what he can get. It is then that he begins to kick . . . and he sits down in his lonely cabin on the bleak prairie and imagines that he is being ground down by the iron heel of monopoly."

*Pioneer Press*
North Dakota

"Here is a tenant—I do not know, or care, whether he is black or white. He starts in and pays $25 for a mule, 1000 pounds of cotton for rent, and two bales for supplies. By the time he pays for that, and the store account, and the guano, he has not enough money left to buy a bottle of laudanum, and not enough cotton to stuff in his old lady's ear."

Tom Watson
Georgia Farmers Alliance Leader

Economic conditions after the Civil War encouraged farmers as well as workers to see themselves as an exploited "producing class."

## FARMERS ALLIANCE SONGS

The farmer is the man who feeds them all
Lives on credit till the fall
With interest rates so high
It's a wonder he don't die
And the mortgage man's the one who gets it all.

There are ninety and nine who live and die
In want and hunger and cold
That one may live in luxury
And be wrapped in a silken fold.
The ninety and nine live in hovels bare
The one is a palace with riches rare
And the one owns cities and houses and lands
And the ninety and nine have empty hands.

The Farmer's Alliance emerged in the 1870s during a period of innovative organizing activity in the rural Midwest and South. Below, a farmer's political rally in Illinois.

**A charter issued in 1881 to a sub-alliance in Haven Township, Kansas.**

were willing to desert the Democrats, "party of their fathers," just as few Northerners were willing to desert the Grand Old Party, which had defended the Union. Only in the frontier states of the Great Plains, particularly Kansas and Texas, did Greenback candidates garner a substantial proportion of the vote.

It was in this atmosphere of agrarian discontent and political experimentation that in 1877 a group of neighbors in Lampasas County, Texas, formed a self-help organization they called the Farmers Alliance. The organization expanded rapidly, forming local chapters known as "sub-alliances" in a dozen nearby counties. But the Alliance, torn by Greenback controversies and uncertain about its goals, was nearly moribund six years after its founding.

In January 1884, the Alliance hired S.O. Daws as its first "travelling lecturer," or professional organizer. Within months, Daws had revived inactive sub-alliances and founded many new ones. At the same time, the organization renewed and deepened its commitment to cooperative marketing and purchasing. County alliances and sub-alliances pursued an array of cooperative strategies, including cooperative cotton warehouses, bulk marketing, Alliance trade stores, and direct purchasing arrangements with manufacturers.

In tandem with Daws' aggressive organizing methods, the cooperative message—join the Alliance and get free of the furnish merchant—produced extraordinary results. By 1886 the Alliance had 100,000 members in 2000 sub-alliances spread across nearly 100 Texas counties. Yet the cooperative experiments encountered severe obstacles. Brokers refused to participate in bulk sales of cotton, merchants sabotaged the Alliance trade stores and warehouses, and no manufacturer would sell directly to Alliance cooperatives.

Stymied by organized commercial resistance to its cooperative schemes, the Alliance gradually relaxed the apolitical stance it had adopted after the debilitating early conflicts over Greenbackism. Delegates to the 1886 Alliance convention in Cleburne drafted a set of demands for government action, including expansion of the national money supply, regulation of railroad rates, taxation of speculative real estate profits, and legal recognition of cooperatives and trade unions. These proposals were controversial; the monetary plank, in particular, clashed with Democratic Party orthodoxy, and the Party still commanded the loyalty of most Texas farmers. When the convention approved the "Cleburne demands" by a 92-75 margin, it set a new and radical course for the Alliance.

One manifestation of the radical mood was a daring proposal by Alliance leader Charles Macune for a State Cooperative Exchange, a central warehouse that would purchase equipment and supplies in bulk and market crops for Alliance members throughout the state. The plan was approved by the Alliance leadership, a site was obtained in Dallas, and Macune began to place supply orders for the 1888 season. But, almost without exception, banks and merchants refused to extend the Exchange

7

**The "Big Store" of the Texas Alliance Cooperative Exchange.**

credit, and it was soon in deep financial distress.

On June 9, 1888—the "day to save the Exchange"—Alliance members rallied at county courthouses throughout Texas to pledge their meager assets to the cooperative. Tens of thousands turned out, pledging some $200,000. The Exchange survived the immediate crisis, but its operations were severely curtailed. This experience and others like it convinced wavering farmers that the cooperative approach could not work without political action to overcome the opposition of "monopoly power."

In the meantime, the farmers movement expanded beyond the Texas borders. Alliance organizers dispatched across the Southern states met with a phenomenal response, while indigenous organizations with strong affinities to the Alliance emerged in some Midwestern and

8

# PEOPLE'S PARTY PAPER.

## "Equal Rights to All—Special Privileges to None."

VOLUME I.      ATLANTA, GA, THURSDAY, FEBRUARY 25, 1892.      NUMBER 22.

### A PLEA FOR JUSTICE.

Showing Up the True Condition and The Cause.

#### HON. THOS. E. WATSON

Gives the House Facts and Figures in Discussing the Indian Appropriation Bill.

Class Legislation Must be Checked or Our Free Institutions are Doomed.

Last Thursday was a lively day in the House. The discussion of the Indian Appropriation bill gave the Reform members a chance to probe the action of past partisan Congresses, and Hon. T. E. Watson got in some good licks for the people's cause. We copy from the Congressional Record:

Mr. Watson. Mr. Chairman, I can not pretend that I am any great admirer of the policy which this Government has pursued with reference to the Indians. I can not see much beauty in taking from the Indian every dollar's worth of property he has got, pinning him down with a bayonet in one corner and feeding him out of a spoon in the hands of an Indian agent. I can not myself say that I admire that to any great extent; but when this Government chooses to go on another line and deal fairly, honorably, and liberally with these people, with a view to bettering their condition, righting wrongs of the past, recognizing the claims that they have upon us, I, for one, Mr. Chairman, shall not be deterred by the condition of my own people from giving my vote to such a policy. [Applause.]

The gentleman from Mississippi [Mr. Stephens] speaks feelingly of the condition of his people. Representing mine, whose condition can not be better, I say, Mr. Chairman, that we ask no stinginess in the treatment of other people, but justice in the treatment of ourselves. Give us fair laws; give us laws which antagonize no special classes; give us laws that confer no special privileges, and we will deal justly with our former slaves on every question; we will deal fairly with the red men on every question; and we will deal fairly with the veterans of the Union army, who upheld the honor of their flag, at the same time that we ask better laws for the one-armed and one-legged veterans who upheld the honor of ours.

Mr. Chairman, I take it for granted that every member upon this floor, while he may differ with his colleagues on individual matters of economy, is at heart a patriot, loves his country, wants to do that thing which is best, and wants to treat every class fairly; wants to know the condition of every class just as it is; and I take it for granted, sir, that in the consideration of these questions, gentlemen will listen patiently to what are the real facts, with a view to reaching proper convictions, which will lead them forward to a support of proper measures.

Mr. Chairman, the day before yesterday the gentleman from Kansas, Farmer Funston, undertook to tell us what the position of the cotton raiser was.

and the improvement of their treatment under the law.

Mr. Chairman, in 1889 we made 6,935,000 bales of cotton. That cotton brought 10¼ cents a pound.

In 1890 we made, not a half million more, as the gentleman from Kansas [Mr. Funston] said, but less than 400,000 more; we made only 7,313,000 bales. It brought us 10 cents a pound. In the year 1891 we made 8,665,000 bales of cotton, bringing us 7 cents per pound. Gentlemen will see that in the past, comparing year with year, there are numbers of years in the catalogue when the increase of the cotton crop over the preceding year was a great deal larger, and when the price, instead of going up, either held its place or went higher.

In 1882 we made only 5,000,000 bales of cotton. In 1883 we made nearly 7,000,000 bales. Yet the price in 1883 was greater than it was in 1882. Going further, Mr. Chairman, I want to say this. The increase of any crop is to be estimated according to the labor employed and upon the area of the land. I can show to Farmer Funston, or farmer anybody else, that the increase

population was 50,000,000. Therefore, there was 1 bale of cotton to every 8.7 persons. In 1890 there was one bale of cotton to every 8.5 persons, and in 1891 nearly the same. Therefore, the net result is this. The fluctuation in the area planted is less than 5 per cent; the fluctuation in the per capita product is less than 6 per cent, while the fluctuation in the price is more than 30 per cent.

Now, Mr. Chairman, that shows the existence of some general cause. What is it? I will not take time to show that the same thing is true about wheat. I will not take time to show that the same thing is true about corn. I might infringe upon somebody's patent right if I were to undertake to speak of corn. [Laughter.] But, Mr. Speaker, I will say this: At the close of the war our national debt was, say, two billions and quarter. We have paid on the principal over a billion dollars; we have paid on the interest over two billion dollars; and yet it would take a greater quantity of corn, it would take a greater quantity of wheat, it would take a greater quantity of cotton to pay the remainder of the public debt now than

years. With half the wealth of the nine states I first named, these twenty-one states have twice the amount of indebtedness.

Now, compare these nine States with the twenty-one States as to land. The twenty-one States contain 985,000 square miles; the nine States only 168 square miles. Therefore, the advantage which these twenty-one agricultural States have over the nine nonagricultural States in that great component part in production—land—is as 6 to 1. Now, how is it as to the other component, labor. In 1880, the population of the twenty-one States was 28,000,000; of the nine States, 14,000,000. Therefore in this respect the twenty-one States had the advantage of the nine States in the proportion of 2 to 1.

Take the other element of production, capital. The nine States had $7,559,000,000; the twenty-one States $6,839,000,000. Therefore in this respect the nine States were ahead of the twenty-one States only a mere fraction. Yet in 1890 the twenty-one States had gained one billion and a half of dollars while the nine States had gained over three billion dollars. Take another

Kansas is underlaid with a layer of rock salt 150 feet thick. Why do we not dig it out and realize wealth from that source? Because we have got no money to invest. According to the last census we have $343,000,000 of indebtedness resting on our State.

Mr. Watson. Mr. Chairman, the State of Georgia, as compared with any other State where protection, monopoly, and classism thrive, has fewer paupers. As compared with any other State where protected industries are in full blast we have fewer criminals, fewer people who are on the vagrant list. I can make this comparison, Mr. Chairman, even with States like New York, Massachusetts, or Pennsylvania, where wealth has accumulated in the hands of a few people while the many go without it. The prosperity of a people lies not so much in the amount of wealth as in the distribution of it.

Now let this comparison which I have made in regard to the State of New York, be made with reference to Pennsylvania or Massachusetts, and the result is the same.

The one State of Pennsylvania gained $12,000,000 more from 1880 to 1890 than

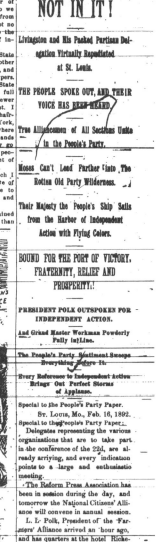

### NOT IN IT !

Livingston and His Packed Partisan Delegation Virtually Repudiated at St. Louis.

#### THE PEOPLE SPOKE OUT, AND THEIR VOICE HAS BEEN HEARD.

True Alliancemen of All Sections Unite in the People's Party.

Moses Can't Lead Further Into The Rotten Old Party Wilderness.

Their Majesty the People's Ship Sails from the Harbor of Independent Action with Flying Colors.

#### BOUND FOR THE PORT OF VICTORY, FRATERNITY, RELIEF AND PROSPERITY!

PRESIDENT POLK OUTSPOKEN FOR INDEPENDENT ACTION.

And Grand Master Workman Powderly Fully in Line.

The People's Party Sentiment Sweeps Everything Before It.

Every Reference to Independent Action Brings Out Perfect Storms of Applause.

Special to the People's Party Paper.

St. Louis, Mo., Feb. 16, 1892. Special to the People's Party Paper:

Delegates representing the various organizations that are to take part in the conference of the 22d, are already arriving, and every indication points to a large and enthusiastic meeting.

The Reform Press Association has been in session during the day, and tomorrow the National Citizens' Alliance will convene in annual session.

L. L. Polk, President of the Farmers' Alliance arrived an hour ago, and has quarters at the hotel Richelieu, where are also quartered the members of the National Committee of the People's Party. This will also be headquarters for the delegates to the Citizens Alliance, which is understood to be an organization strongly favoring independent political action, and these facts taken together are construed as meaning that Polk is for independent action himself;

**GATHERING OF THE CLANS—ON TO WASHINGTON. (VIA ST. LOUIS.)**

We are coming brother toilers, we will trust in rogues no more;
We have buried all dead issues and old grudges of the war;
We have bridged the "bloody chasm," and we'll bury out of sight

All the thieves and thugs in office who have trampled on the right,
Ho! Brothers, "up and at them!" let us once again be free—
Cast out the plotting devils and drive them in the sea.

Upper Plains states. A white minister and Alliance activist, R.M. Humphrey, founded a separate order known as the Colored Farmers Alliance, which an interracial corps of organizers quietly spread through the black communities of the South.

Between 1889 and 1892, a series of national meetings and conventions knit together the diverse strands of the farmers movement. These meetings were dominated by two topics. One was the evolution of a national program, which emerged in its definitive form at the Omaha Convention of 1892. The Omaha Platform emphasized the same three issues as the Cleburne demands six years earlier—land, transportation, and monetary policy—and many of the planks were unchanged. Among the differences were the substitution of government ownership of the railroads for government regulation, and the addition of planks calling for a federal income tax and direct election of U.S. Senators. The most significant innovation was Charles Macune's "sub-treasury" plan, a nationwide network of public banks, which would have simultaneously generated low-interest cash loans to farmers and a vast increase in the supply of money.

The political strategy of the movement was the subject of constant debate. By this point the farmers were deeply involved in electoral politics at the state and local level. Organizations in the Midwestern states had sponsored independent slates in the 1890 elections, while throughout the South the Alliance had endorsed Democrats pledged to support the farmers' demands. The question was whether to form a third party at the national level.

Initially, the Midwesterners, the Colored Farmers Alliance, and some Texas "radicals" advocated a third party strategy, while the bulk of the white Southerners were reluctant to break with the Democrats. But the Southerners were eventually won over, swayed by the weak legislative performance of many "Alliance Demo-crats," the radical momentum of the farmers' movement, and the growing commitment of Alliance members to Macune's sub-treasury plan, which was anathema to the "sound money" ideologists of the national Democratic Party.

In 1892, the new People's Party ran candidates for U.S. President and Vice-President and numerous state and local offices. The Populists, as they had come to be known, scored victories throughout the South and West, electing five U.S. Senators and 10 Congressmen, and gaining control of the Kansas state government. But the Party was unable to make significant inroads among the urban workers of the North, despite support from Knights of Labor assemblies and other local unions. Labor organizations were too weak and too divided to constitute an electoral base comparable to the farmers alliances.

Nevertheless, the success of the People's Party prompted vicious counter-attacks. Republican bosses in the North and West "waved the bloody shirt of rebellion," characterizing the new party as a Democratic front; Democratic bosses in the South stirred up racism among poor whites to win them back to the party of their fathers. Southern blacks who attempted to vote were frequently attacked and occasionally murdered; their ballots often went uncounted.

Success also attracted political opportunists to the People's Party, along with silver mine owners who stood to gain from the Party's call for unlimited silver coinage, a longstanding but heretofore minor element of the Populist monetary program. In states such as Nebraska, Colorado, and Illinois, where the Alliance was weak, silver interests and their allies built their own People's Party organization and financed candidates who were not committed to the Omaha Platform. At the same time, the silver interests were penetrating the Democratic Party, exploiting grassroots disaffection with the disastrous monetary policies of Democratic President Grover Cleve-

**Kansas Populists won control of the state legislature in the 1892 election but had to display armed force to defend their rightful place in the legislative chambers.**

## ALLIANCE WOMEN

**"Raise less corn and more hell,"** preached fiery Mary Lease, one of the most prominent Populist orators.

A significant number of Alliance activists were farmwives and daughters. **"The Alliance has come to redeem woman from her enslaved condition,"** declared one Texas member. **"She is admitted into the organization as an equal of her brother."**

Some women, however, complained that they were only valued for their contributions to picnics or similar functions. And, though leadership was theoretically open to both sexes, men occupied nearly all the elected posts.

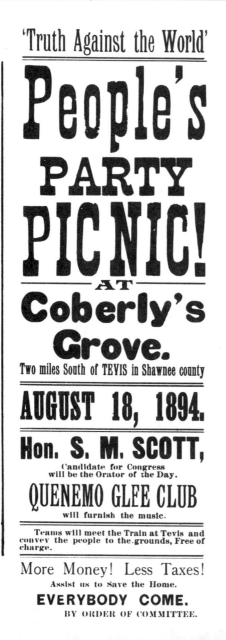

## 'Truth Against the World'

# People's PARTY PICNIC!

### AT

# Coberly's Grove.

Two miles South of TEVIS in Shawnee county

# AUGUST 18, 1894.

# Hon. S. M. SCOTT,

Candidate for Congress will be the Orator of the Day.

# QUENEMO GLEE CLUB

will furnish the music.

Teams will meet the Train at Tevis and convey the people to the grounds, Free of charge.

More Money! Less Taxes!

Assist us to Save the Home.

**EVERYBODY COME.**

BY ORDER OF COMMITTEE.

11

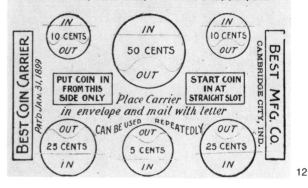

**Headquarters Peoples Party of Kansas.**
Topeka, Kansas.

Dear Friend and Comrade:-

The battle is now on. The forces are in battle array. Every force at our command is being called into play. We have the spirit, the will, the enthusiasm, and everything necessary to give us a glorious victory, except finances.

We have no state institutions to bleed, and we have no giant corporation to contribute to our treasury. The privileged classes are against us. We are, as we ever have been, dependent for the sinews of war, upon the plain, common people; and it is to them that we are now appealing. This card is a messenger to you, and a call for help. Send it back to us very soon, with as much as you can spare. Every little helps. Do your part and the victory is ours. *1902*

Yours in the fight,

W. J. BABB, Chairman,    J. H. CURRAN, Sec.

12

**Far from tearing down the pillars of the two-party system, the silver crusade destroyed the Populist alternative.**

land. For Democrats, a pro-silver position became a means of protesting the extremes of "sound money" without embracing the radical tenets of the Populists.

After the election of 1894, which brought setbacks for the People's Party in the West, Party silverites argued that the only route to victory on a national scale was an electoral coalition or "fusion" with disaffected Democrats around the silver issue.

This fusion strategy rested on the abandonment of the Omaha Platform, which was too radical a document for most Democrats to swallow. The Alliance veterans who still dominated the Populist leadership vehemently opposed dilution of the platform. But the fusionists were gaining influence, and they gradually yoked the Party to the silver crusade.

The Democrats confounded the Populists' expectations in 1896 by nominating William Jennings Bryan, a Nebraska silverite, as their candidate for President. With the Democrats making silver the centerpiece of their campaign, the fusionists contended there was little choice but to nominate Bryan as well. In a chaotic and bitterly divided People's Party convention, the fusionists prevailed.

Bryan's watered-down version of Populism didn't work; he lost the election to Republican William McKinley, whose campaign was generously financed by banks and large corporations. The outcome was widely perceived as a crushing defeat for Populism. But the defeat had actually occurred earlier, in the chain of events leading to the 1896 People's Party convention. When the Party abandoned the Omaha Platform, it abandoned its radical heritage and its reason for being. And when the poor farmers lost control of the party they had built, they lost not only a mighty vehicle for change, but the hope that had sustained it.

# The Nonpartisan League

After the demise of the Farmers Alliance, agrarian grievances against the railroad and brokerage monopolies did not abate, particularly in the "Wheat Belt" states of the Great Plains. Farmers continued to attempt cooperative enterprises and to support reform candidates for public office. In 1907, another ambitious farmers organization took shape. Called the American Society of Equity, it was built on a simple premise: Join the Equity and we will raise the price of wheat.

The plan was to band together and pledge to hold wheat off the market until the price was driven up by short supplies. For four years, the Equity claimed success, but in reality the tactic was unworkable. Farmers simply couldn't afford to wait to sell their crops because mortgage payments came due soon after the harvest.

The Equity was in trouble and its leaders devised a new strategy to revive it. They organized a vigorous campaign to establish a cooperative grain terminal in Minneapolis where farmers could store and sell their wheat. By 1913, membership had grown to 40,000.

In North Dakota, where the Equity was strong, politics was dominated by a few powerful figures with ties to the grain brokers in Minnesota. Together, they tried to drive the Equity Cooperative Exchange out of business, employing a potent combination of newspaper attacks and legal harassment. The controversy taught North Dakota farmers that their fight was not only with far-off financial interests in the Twin Cities but with elected officials at home, setting the stage for a more politicized farmers movement.

The potential was seized not by the leadership of the Equity but by a group of local Socialist Party activists led by A.C. Townley, a failed flax farmer. Townley had been involved in a short-lived Party experiment known as the

SOME LEAKS IN THE PIPE LINE

"Organization Department." The idea had been to enlist farmers by highlighting the Party's relatively moderate and popular platform without trying to convert them to Socialism. Despite instant success, the Organization Department was shut down for fear that it would dilute the ideological commitment of the Party. Townley and his associates, however, had gained valuable experience which they applied to building an organization they named the Nonpartisan League (NPL).

Rather than following the third party strategy that had proven unsuccessful for the Farmers Alliance and the Socialists, the NPL took a new approach. Direct primaries had recently been instituted as the mechanism for selecting party candidates for office. Instead of running on an independent ticket, candidates pledged to the League platform would enter Republican and Democratic primaries. This strategy allowed insurgent candidates to exploit the voters' traditional party loyalties rather than foundering on them. A candidate with a well-organized

Leaders of the American Society of Equity, above, and the Socialist Party of North Dakota, below. The Nonpartisan League activated the Equity's farm membership base with a political reform program derived from the Socialists.

**15**

"The mission of the League is to unite the farmers of this state, regardless of past party affiliations, into an organization that will stand apart from every political party . . . and free from every political boss, and put men in office that will legislate in the interests of the members of that organization."

*Nonpartisan Leader*
January 6, 1916

**16**

NPL Headquarters, Bismarck, ND.

17

bloc of supporters could win the primary and obtain the nomination without the support of the party bosses, and then count on the votes of party loyalists in the general election.

The state legislature provided a catalyst for the fledgling organization. In l915, lawmakers ignored the results of a statewide referendum and voted against the establishment of a state-owned grain elevator. Legend has it that when Equity members protested the decision they were told to "go home and slop the hogs."

The incident provided fertile ground for the League's political agenda. Organizers, trained in sales psychology and outfitted with Model T's, fanned out across the state. Many of their first members came from Equity locals and some served as "boosters," introducing NPL organizers to their neighbors. Sometimes, the organizer brought along a farmhand who would take the farmer's place at the plow while the organizer explained the League platform.

Members paid $6 dues, later raised to $16 biannually, and promised to support League candidates for public office. In February 1916, the League laid the groundwork for the spring primaries. At simultaneous precinct caucuses, 26,000 members chose delegates to district and state conventions where nominees for public office would be selected. As a test of organizational strength, the caucuses were a notable success; dozens reported 100 percent turnout and not one meeting had fewer than 90 percent of League members present.

In March, the first NPL state convention in Fargo opened with a mass rally and parade of 2000 farmers. The 45 official delegates proceeded to name a slate of candidates for statewide office. With the exception of its Supreme Court nominees, every candidate was a bona fide farmer. All but one would run in the majority Republican Party primary, but of the 98 legislative candidates chosen at district conventions, 21 were Democrats and two were Socialists.

Spring planting delayed campaigning until June, when a series of all-day picnics demonstrated enthusiastic support for the League slate. In one county, half the population turned out. Violent storms on primary day did not deter NPL voters; the entire statewide slate and three-fourths of the legislative candidates won nomination.

The primary victories carried over to the November general election; all but one League candidate for statewide office was elected, the NPL gained solid control of the House and took 18 of the 25 open Senate seats. Nonpartisanship held; in districts where League candidates ran on opposing tickets, voters crossed party lines to elect both Republicans and Democrats endorsed by the NPL.

Two years later, the League repeated its stunning electoral performance and gained effective control of the state government. Many parts of the League platform became reality. The legislature established a state flour mill to give farmers a better price for their wheat and a state-owned bank to make farm loans available. It exempted improvements to farm property from taxation and extended the state hail insurance program.

Opposition intensified from the economic interests the League had displaced from power. Detractors could not openly attack the substance of the popular NPL platform. Instead, they attacked the integrity of League leaders and officeholders, accusing them of using dues money for personal gain. Although the League was putatively

18

The League employed traveling organizers who earned a salary plus commission on the dues they collected.

Certificate of Membership
in
The National Nonpartisan League

This Certifies that _____ is a member in good standing in The National Nonpartisan League and is entitled to participate in Conventions and other gatherings of the League with full privileges as such member

The National Nonpartisan League

Date of joining _____ 191__

This certificate good to December 1st 1918.

A. C. Townley
NATIONAL PRESIDENT

19

20

"Lord, what a meeting! Big opera house, lots of seats, and yet twenty-five people stood up for one hour forty-five minutes. Local banker said that never in the history of Edmore had he seen so many rigs as were here today.

Even after the meeting the enthusiasm did not wane. Crowds met the speaker on the street and shook his hand and sent messages of good cheer to the boys at headquarters. 'Tell them they're all right and playing a great game. This time we'll get something! If they need more money we've got that too.'

It was reported on the street that a prominent politician had said, 'The League had the state all sewed up in a bag.' The report spread like wildfire and everybody was happy."

letter from an Edmore, ND farmer to the *Nonpartisan Leader*

democratic, its three top leaders, Townley, William Lemke, and F.B. Wood, were not always accountable to the membership. They invested NPL funds in shaky financial ventures, which supplied ammunition to efforts to discredit the organization. Internal splits developed and some statewide officials elected with NPL endorsement defected.

League opponents also took advantage of the nationalistic atmosphere which flourished during and immediately after World War I, painting the NPL as a subversive organization tied to Bolshevism and "free love." As evidence, they cited the Socialist background of Townley and other leaders as well as the League's opposition to U.S. participation in the war. The impact of the war issue is questionable, since anti-war and anti-British sentiments were endemic in rural North Dakota, particularly among farmers of German and Irish descent. But the "Red Scare" which developed in the wake of the 1917

Russian Revolution undoubtedly created a more difficult political environment for the League.

Flushed with its early success, the League had sent organizers outside North Dakota, and by 1919 claimed 300,000 members in 20 midwestern and western states. Where the organization did not dominate state politics, it faced more violent opposition. In Minnesota, local officials and vigilante mobs routinely broke up NPL meetings. Organizers were beaten and arrested; Townley ultimately served 90 days in a Minnesota jail on charges of conspiring to discourage Army enlistments.

On the homefront in North Dakota, an effective rival group called the Independent Voters Association (IVA) was organized, and the League lost some ground in the 1920 elections. In 1921, the IVA succeeded in removing some NPL representatives from office through a special election, claiming they had mismanaged the state businesses. Ironically, the recall mechanism had been es-

# BATTLE
# OF THE
# CARTOONISTS

Within a few months of its first publication in September 1915, the *Nonpartisan Leader* was the largest circulation newspaper in North Dakota, providing a direct means of communication with League members and a forum to combat the opposition's attacks. The newspaper was noted for political cartoons drawn by John Miller Baer, who continued as its cartoonist after his election to the U.S. Congress.

22

23

tablished as part of the NPL's reform program.

The League never fully recovered. Thrown on the defensive by its opponents and unable to replicate its North Dakota victories in other states, its grassroots momentum dissipated. The League became a more conventional political organization, helping to swing elections in the 1920s, '30s, and '40s to reform-minded candidates such as Lemke, Lynn Frazier, "Wild Bill" Langer, and Jeanette Rankin, the first woman elected to the U.S. Congress.

Political formations, like the Minnesota Democratic-Farmer-Labor Party, remain as evidence of a distinctive Midwestern progressive tradition molded by agrarian insurgencies. And the brief flowering of a farmers' commonwealth left an enduring legacy to the League's native state: the North Dakota Mill and the Bank of North Dakota, unique publicly-owned enterprises which are still doing business today.

The state-owned North Dakota mill, still in operation, is a testament to the sweeping impact of the Nonpartisan League during its brief moment in power.

21

The *Red Flame* was a short-lived anti-League monthly begun in 1919. Its shrewd cartoons depicted League leaders as villainous ideologues.

## The Southern Tenant Farmers Union

By the 1930s, the crop lien system had forced the majority of Southern farmers—white and black—into tenant farming or "sharecropping." When debts to the furnishing merchant became insupportable, farmers lost title to their land but stayed on as tenants, owing the landlord up to half their crop at harvest plus, oftentimes, the cost of supplies at interest rates as high as 40 percent. Since cotton was the only sure cash crop, tenant farmers were prohibited from growing anything else.

Sharecroppers were further devastated by the Great Depression. In 1933, President Franklin D. Roosevelt signed a relief measure, the Agricultural Adjustment Act, which required farmers to plow up one-third of their cotton in order to drive up farm prices. The farmers were

26　　**A sharecropper family evicted from an Arkansas plantation, 1936.**

**Picnic and mass meeting of the Shady Grove local, STFU, near Forrest City, AR.**

paid compensation for the crops they destroyed and tenants were supposed to receive a share. But federal payments went to the landlords, who frequently kept the whole amount. With production limited, many planters no longer needed the labor of their tenants and evicted them. Between a half a million and a million farmers were displaced by the crop reduction program in two years.

The distress of the sharecroppers in Eastern Arkansas aroused two rural radicals— H.L. Mitchell, a dry cleaner, and his neighbor, Clay East, a gas station owner—who founded the Southern Tenant Farmers Union. They initially set out to organize an Arkansas chapter of the Socialist Party and invited Norman

"We called it the system. You guys called it the power structure. It's all the same. See, we made an inroad with the whites and blacks here. We had done something that none of these agrarian movements had really done. They had all floundered on this race thing. But we didn't. We didn't flounder on it. We held our principles."

H.L. Mitchell
Executive Secretary, STFU

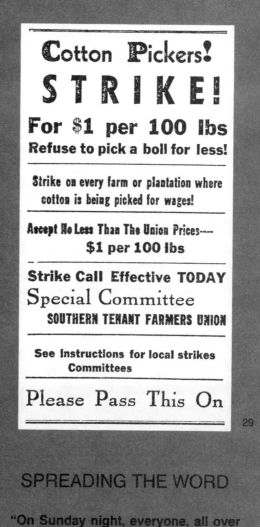

# Cotton Pickers!
# STRIKE!
## For $1 per 100 lbs
### Refuse to pick a boll for less!

Strike on every farm or plantation where cotton is being picked for wages!

Accept No Less Than The Union Prices----
$1 per 100 lbs

## Strike Call Effective TODAY
## Special Committee
### SOUTHERN TENANT FARMERS UNION

See Instructions for local strikes Committees

## Please Pass This On

## SPREADING THE WORD

"On Sunday night, everyone, all over Arkansas where there was an organization alive, had to be on the job at eleven passing out leaflets ... I was riding in my car . . . I was laying down on my stomach holding the door cracked open, and I'd push the leaflets through the crack and spread them out in the street. You pick up speed and that'd just make them things go flying all over the yards.

Then this car came swooping by us. I said, 'Cut the lights and let's go right into these woods' . . . If they had caught us, I don't know what they would've done to us . . . Water was up to our knees in the car. It was three o'clock that next morning when we got home and it was still raining. It wasn't no easy job. White folks thought a plane had flown over there and spread all them leaflets. They were all over the state."

Carrie Dillworth
STFU leader

30

**Meeting to plan National Sharecroppers Week: (from left) STFU member Beatrice Johnson, STFU president J.R. Butler, New York Mayor Fiorello LaGuardia, and Harriet M. Young, secretary, National Sharecroppers Week.**

"It was the major role of the union to bring in outside support, money, etc. It had to be. It was the only way we could survive. The members didn't have enough money to pay dues to the organization for it to operate."

George Stith
STFU vice-president

**Norman Thomas addresses an STFU rally in Bay Ridge, AR, 1937.**

31

Thomas, the Party's presidential candidate, to speak in their hometown of Tyronza. As East recalls, "The way the union got started, when Norman Thomas came to speak we had dinner at my home and during the meal Norman was the first one that planted that idea in our heads. He told me, 'What you need here is a union.'"

J.R. Butler, who later served as president, describes the beginning of the union in July 1934: "I can't remember just how many there were at the first meeting but as I remember it was about fifty-fifty, about half white and half black. We had to have an understanding among the union members and you couldn't have much understanding if you had two separate unions." The STFU's commitment to an integrated union was principled but pragmatic; where necessary, there were dual locals. However, all important actions were decided at integrated meetings and the leadership was racially balanced. The objective was not racial "progress" but the elimination of race as an obstacle to building the union.

The STFU utilized a strong identification with religion, quoting Scriptures in speeches, meeting in churches, and recruiting preachers as organizers. The story told by Myrtle Moskop, a white sharecropper, is not unusual: "I was just like all the other people in Wynne. When they first started talking about union, I thought it was a new church." One of the most common protest anthems to this day, "We Shall Not Be Moved," was adapted by an STFU member from a popular hymn.

The union first sought federal redress of sharecroppers' grievances. In December 1934, a delegation occupied U.S. Secretary of Agriculture Henry Wallace's office until he promised an investigation. Then, at a rally in the town square of Marked Tree, called to celebrate the federal investigation, a young white minister and union organizer named Ward Rodgers was arrested for criminal anarchy. More arrests followed, along with church burnings, beatings, and murder attempts, as the planters and their allies unleashed a campaign of intimidation against the STFU.

Rodgers' arrest became a cause celebre among Northern liberals, Socialists, churches, and Negro organizations. Big-city newspapers carried stirring accounts of the sharecroppers' plight and the "reign of terror" in Arkansas. The most important benefit of this publicity was financial. Dues never amounted to much income for the STFU; only $500 was collected in 1935. But welcome contributions arrived from religious denominations, philanthropists, and special defense funds which sprang up in major cities.

The violence drove union headquarters out of Tyronza to Memphis, Tennessee. Open meetings were suspended and Mitchell prepared pamphlets for organizers warning them to "go quietly, not more than two or three together, not to go the main routes always, but go the back roads." The union newspaper, *Sharecroppers Voice*, appealed to members to maintain a nonviolent stance.

When the federal government did not intervene and its eagerly awaited investigation was suppressed, the STFU took a different tack. Like industrial workers, the tenant farmers calculated that their greatest power rested in withholding labor. The quality of cotton suffers if it is not harvested at the proper time; by refusing to pick the cotton, the union hoped to raise wages and win recognition.

The first general strike in 1935 was tightly organized. At 11 o'clock the night before, members delivered strike handbills all over Arkansas, Missouri, and parts of Tennessee, Mississippi, and Alabama. Not daring to picket, 5000 cotton pickers simply stayed home the next morning. The landlords capitulated, boosting the prevailing wage from less than 50 cents per 100 pounds to 75 cents or more. The union grew dramatically after the strike; 30 new locals were organized within 45 days.

But the STFU was unable to win recognition as the bargaining agent for sharecroppers. One planter who had agreed to sign a contract was threatened with foreclosure by his bank if he did not evict the union members from his plantation. He complied and the STFU organized a

**Members of the Oklahoma Tenant Farmers Union at a Muskegee schoolhouse, 1939.**

Organizers

( 1935.3(

Who can become an organizer for STFU.?---Any member who is in good standing who has the necessary qualifications.
What are the qualifications?    First to become a successful organizer a member must know the fundementals of the organization---he must be level headed---he does not have to be a forceful speaker--some men can do both speak and build organization---many good speakers have no ability to organize a group of men into a working body.
How shall I start organizing?---First get a number of good men in the particula -r community where you wish to organize---a small number 10 or 15 at most is the best number to start with---Have them meet quietly after they have decided to become members---at one the potential members houses---have them sign an application for a charter ---elect Pres-Vice Pres--Secretary--report this to National Office the next day.  Have them understand the responsibility for growth of the Union depends on them---put them to work building the organ -ization.   They can explain to the people what we are trying to do.
Your Job isn't to convert the whole neigborhood including the planters but to get a real working union built.----Do not have a big meeting with sneaks and pets out to tell every thing that is said and lot that isn't.
Build the Union a small organized unit is worth ten times more than a hundred members who scarecely know what it is about.
First build organization---give them a start they will do the work after you are gone and after they have a large organization working well they can have good speakers--let them arrange it thru their Secretary--who will take the matter up thru the proper channels.

Help the men select good officers--get a Secretary who can read and write keep a fair record of what goes on--and above all one who will answer letters Elect a President who can keep order--elect officials who want to do something. You canhelp the men elect the officers--by suggesting who will make good ones.


Collect from each member fee for membership book-5¢ each---the initiation fee is the organizers---collect what you can take note of the one who promise to pay you and the time that he will pay it---don't turn members down who can't pay the initiation fee---but make it clearly understood that each months dues must be paid--and the cost of the membership book must be paid if we are going to have a union.

Explain the low dues---10 ¢ per month---4¢ to Community Council--2 ¢ County organization 4¢ National Organization.   These are to be handled by stamps the Secretary will order them paying ####6¢  #####################################
each they will be sold to members for 10¢---4¢ will be used for Union expenses only.

Do your work quietly---a great deal of publicity will not build the Union ---Get the organization built up---first them let the membership arrange for big meetings with speakers.

roadside encampment to draw attention to the situation. Planters retaliated by blacklisting workers, and the camp was dynamited.

Continued violence and the resultant national publicity finally compelled government authorities to respond. The governor of Arkansas established a Commission on Farm Tenancy, later replicated at the federal level. Both commissions recommended programs to "enable those who cultivate the soil to own the land." Part of their stated rationale was to stymie Communist and Socialist organizing by giving "dispossessed people a stake in the social system."

The STFU maintained that land ownership alone would not protect its members from exploitation. Instead, it advocated cooperative agricultural communities and created the Delta Cooperative Farm in Mississippi as a model. The union's position was based both on a cooperative vision and on the practical view that very small farms were not economically viable.

Congress eventually adopted a farm relief bill that authorized loans for land purchase by the landless. However, the program was limited to a few hundred counties, permitted no more than 10 loans per county, and granted veto power to local committees composed of established farmers. A more significant product of the relief legislation was the Farm Security Administration (FSA), which aided close to a million farm families and established several coop farms in Mississippi and Arkansas.

Among the FSA's projects was the Delmo Labor Homes, built in response to the last major STFU protest. In January 1939, 1700 sharecroppers were evicted by Southeast Missouri landlords seeking to evade a new federal rule requiring them to share compensation payments with their tenants. STFU organizers set up a tent city along Highways 60 and 61. The governor ordered relief, Secretary Wallace promised to withhold payments from the landlords, and President Roosevelt agreed to send the National Guard to help. Before any of this aid arrived, local police moved the evicted sharecroppers to a swampy "concentration camp" away from the public eye. The FSA dispatched relief checks and ultimately relocated the displaced sharecroppers to Delmo Homes.

A scene from the Delta Cooperative Farm in Mississippi, an STFU experiment in collective agriculture. The interracial coop survived until the 1950s when segregationists forced it to close.

Police disband a roadside tent city erected by homeless sharecroppers in Southeast Missouri.

**Tenant farm leaders of a CIO local, Creek County, OK. The STFU affiliated with the Cannery Workers in the late 1930s but the marriage did not create a viable organization.**

By this time, the union was suffering from severe internal conflicts generated by a problematic affiliation with the United Cannery, Agricultural, Packing and Allied Workers of America, CIO. The STFU ultimately disaffiliated but was decimated in the process. Mitchell recounts that, "in 1937, when we joined the CIO, we had more than 200 locals. . .and when we wound up in that battle. . .we had about 30 or 40 locals, just a handful of people." Neither the CIO nor the AFL would make a serious commitment to organize farmworkers. The AFL's rejection was pointed: "There did not appear to be a financial basis for the organization of a trade union among sharecroppers."

The era of the sharecropper was, indeed, almost over. As the agriculture system of the South was mechanized, the economic rationale for the "system" collapsed. World War II and the postwar boom created an intense demand for industrial labor, which was filled by a stream of migrants from the rural South. In one of its final actions, the STFU helped more than 10,000 displaced farmworkers find jobs at food packing plants in the North and on the West Coast.

Some sectors of American agriculture, notably fruit and vegetable growers, continued to rely on low-wage agricultural labor, often supplied by migrant workers. Mitchell persisted in organizing farmworkers in California and Louisiana, but the mainstream of American labor showed little interest. Finally, in the 1960s, the AFL-CIO put its weight behind a new drive led by Cesar Chavez to organize fruit and vegetable pickers on the West Coast. Like the STFU, the United Farm Workers harnessed press coverage and public opinion to its cause, generating a broad-based national boycott and support movement akin to the sharecroppers' crusade in the 1930s. But unlike its predecessor, the UFW won recognition from large growers and built a secure membership base, realizing the dream of an agricultural union which the founders of the STFU had articulated so boldly a generation before.

**A farmworkers picket in California. The 1965 strike in the Delano vineyards produced precedent-setting contracts and, with the merger of Cesar Chavez's Farm Workers Association and the AFL-CIO's Agricultural Workers Organizing Committee, the first durable farmworkers union.**

**THE LABOR STRUGGLE**

# The Knights of Labor

The Noble and Holy Order of the Knights of Labor collapsed nearly a century ago. Yet, despite its archaic name, the Knights of Labor was the first truly national labor organization and the first to grasp the shape of a new economic order.

The post-Civil War economic transformation that squeezed U.S. farmers had similar effects on industrial workers. Mechanization, periodic depressions, a tide of immigration, and the sheer size of the new corporate enterprises combined to erode the bargaining position of labor. Conditions in the new factories and mines were dangerous and unhealthy. Wages were so low that entire families, including children as young as six, worked 12 or even 16 hours a day to earn a bare subsistence income.

Workers in such skilled crafts as bricklaying, carpentry, and shoemaking had long been organized into unions. But craft-based unions were increasingly ineffectual confronting industries which spanned dozens of trades. Many labor leaders recognized the need to link workers across trade lines and experimented with a variety of organizational forms. In 1866, prominent craft unionists launched an ambitious attempt to create a National Trade Union. The effort failed, but an organization of more modest origins, the Knights of Labor, succeeded. Led by Uriah Stephens, eight members of a failing garment cutters union in Philadelphia formed the Knights in 1869. Stephens declared his determination "to originate something that will be different from what we have ever had."

The Knights borrowed some traditions from their predecessors. Like the guilds which craftsmen had formed since the Middle Ages for mutual protection and social purposes, the Knights employed secret rituals, handshakes, and signs. Secrecy fostered solidarity among the members but its primary function was practical—to avoid reprisals from employers. Even the name of the organization was kept secret at first; five asterisks were used in its place.

The Knights also continued the guild practice of using their meetings to educate members on the news of the day and to share songs, essays and poems they had written. Self-improvement was encouraged; in keeping with the Order's promotion of literacy, each member was required to sign his name before entering a lodge. In place of the saloons customarily located on the ground floor of workingman's halls, the order established cooperative stores. Through such practices, the Knights strived to create enclaves of "workingman's culture" which would enhance the status and self-respect of labor.

The Order broke sharply with the craft union tradition in its commitment to organize workers across trade lines, regardless of race, sex, nationality, or level of skill. This idealistic philosophy was rooted in Stephens'
Quaker upbringing, Baptist ministerial studies, and abolitionist activities, as well as his recognition that trade unions were too narrow in scope to counter the concentration of capital. The universal approach he advocated offered the Knights strategic advantages. By organizing all the workers in an industry rather than selected craftsmen, the union could shut down whole factories or mines. And by organizing entire communities, it could call general strikes and boycotts to pressure employers.

**Leaders of the Knights of Labor.**

At first the Order grew slowly. By 1877, there were District Assemblies centered in Camden, New Jersey, and in Philadelphia and Pittsburgh, Pennsylvania. That year, a major strike broke out on the B&O railroad, which soon spread to transportation systems throughout the nation. Local militias were called out to quell the strike but soldiers often sided with the workers instead. After several bloody battles the strike was crushed, but a new spirit of labor unity and militance had been born.

Though the Knights hadn't organized the strike, they benefited from the new impetus for unionism, expanding westward into Ohio, Indiana, West Virginia, and Illinois; and north to Massachusetts and New York. On January 1, 1878, the Order held its first convention and adopted a national structure and platform. Over the next five years, the union grew from 9000 to nearly 60,000 members.

In 1885, the Order conducted a successful strike against railroad "robber baron" Jay Gould. Defeating the most notorious popular symbol of monopoly enhanced the Knights' prestige, and membership soared. More as-

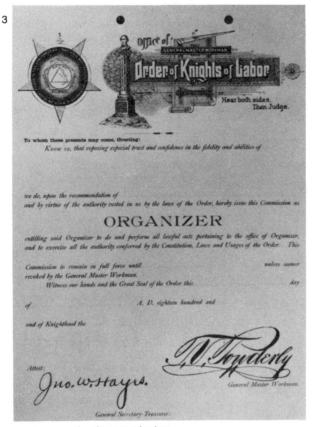

An organizer's commission.

Secret practices served both functional and ritual purposes. Left, miners call a meeting by chalking a signal on a rock. Right, interior diagram of a Knights' lodge.

semblies were formed in the following year than in the previous 16. After 515 assemblies were organized in the month of February alone, recruitment was suspended for 40 days to allow time for consolidation.

The union ultimately reached a membership of nearly one million with assemblies in every state and territory. It had members in all but a dozen of the country's 400 major urban centers and a strong rural base as well, drawn initially from mining communities and later from Southern farm labor. Most of the Order's early members belonged to Local Assemblies which were organized along separate trade lines but were linked at the district, state, and national levels with other trades. By 1886, however, half the members belonged to Mixed Assemblies that combined different occupations in the same workplace or many trades within the same community.

In the face of widespread prejudice, the Knights did not shrink from organizing women and minorities. Their platform held that both sexes should receive equal pay for equal work. In the mid-1880s, women in the Northeastern textile and garment industries demonstrated their militancy and perseverance in a number of successful strikes, and in 1886 the Order established a separate Department of Women's Work under the direction of Leonora Barry, a widowed hosiery worker with two small children.

Barry's work was hampered by employers' efforts to pit men against women, sometimes enticing men to break

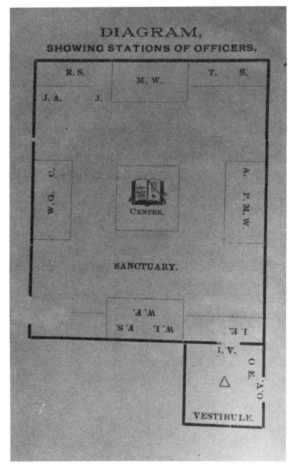

strikes with offers of higher wages. An equally difficult obstacle was the attitude of women themselves. "Many women are deterred from joining labor organizations by foolish pride, prudish modesty, and religious scruples," Barry found. "A prevailing cause is the hope. . .that in the near future marriage will lift them out of the industrial life and into the quiet and comfort of a home. . .often finding, however, that their struggle has only begun when they have to go back to the shop for two instead of one."

The Knights demonstrated their commitment to racial justice at the 1886 national convention in Richmond, Virginia. Black delegate Frank Farrell of New York was refused lodging in any hotel so his entire assembly prepared to camp out for the night. Farrell was given the honor of introducing the Knights' chief officer, Grand Master Workman Terence V. Powderly, to the convention. Later, his assembly integrated the Richmond opera house for the first time.

Bowing to Southern custom, many local assemblies were segregated. But Knights broke the color line in Louisville, Birmingham, and Dallas with public rallies addressed by both black and white leaders; and the Order was integrated at the district and national levels. Despite frequent equivocation on the issue of racial unity, the · Knights of Labor was the only 19th century labor union to actively recruit blacks; in 1886, they constituted ten percent of the membership.

The Knights advocated the eight-hour day; weekly

## A REPORT FROM THE FIELD

"I confess that it was with some misgivings I left home upon the mission, but such were soon dispelled on my arrival and an exchange of greetings with the applicants for a charter. I found a body of men who in intelligence, social standing, morals, etc. compare very favorably with any body of organized labor. I find that they have no ulterior motive of using force in any way except such as is exerted by intelligent, conservative action in the common welfare of the working masses. I remained with them three evenings and posted and drilled them well in the work of a Local Assembly."

A.A. Beaton, District Master Workman
Report to the General Executive Board, 1888

pay in cash; health and safety legislation; a prohibition on child labor under 15 years of age; a graduated income tax; government ownership of railroads, telegraphs, and telephones; and other laws to hold monopolies in check. Their ultimate goal was to create a "cooperative commonwealth" that would supercede the wage system and "secure to the workers the full enjoyment of the wealth they create."

Toward this end, the Knights experimented, like the Farmers Alliance, with a range of cooperative enterprises. The most common form was the store set up on the first floor of the Order's lodges. Other businesses grew out of strike efforts, reflecting the leadership's preference to invest in self-help ventures rather than costly strike funds. The "cooperative commonwealth" was more ideal than reality, however, as most efforts were unsuccessful, in part because banks and suppliers refused to do business with them.

The ideal of cooperation extended to the Order's view of the proper relations between labor and capital. Its Declaration of Principles called for arbitration between workers and employers "in order that the bonds of sympathy between them may be strengthened and that strikes may be rendered unnecessary."

Nonetheless, local assemblies engaged in countless work stoppages—often without the support of the national union—in pursuit of higher wages, shorter hours, and better working conditions. The Knights also organized consumer and supplier boycotts to provide leverage on anti-union employers. While boycotts were a common union tactic in the 19th century, often employed as an alternative to the more risky strike, the Knights' broad community base made the tactic particularly effective. Circulars and handbills kept members informed of the extensive array of products and businesses to avoid, and the adoption of a "union label" affixed to union-made products aided the process.

In 1885, the Knights registered 196 boycotts aimed at hats, cigars, clothing, shoes, stoves, flour, beer, pianos, and newspapers. "Secondary" boycotts, directed at those who did business with the primary target, could take creative forms. In a boycott against Berg's hat factory in Orange, New Jersey, for instance, brewers refused to furnish beer to bars frequented by Berg's strikebreakers.

One of the Knights' most celebrated but disastrous strikes was the 1886 action against Gould's Southwestern railroads. Gould was not content to let the union's victory of the year before stand; he precipitated the strike by firing a Texas Knight for attending a District Assembly meeting. The walkout quickly spread to all of Gould's holdings, with union recognition and a dollar-a-day wage increase as the central demands. Pitched battles took place between strikers and militiamen; scores were killed and hundreds jailed on sabotage and other charges.

Rank and file sentiment compelled the national leadership to support the strike, but Powderly soon at-

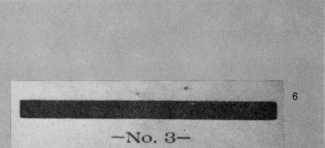

## —No. 3—
# A BLACK LIST

Of patrons of the Daily Gazette being boycotted by Wabash Assembly K. of L., and the Trades and Labor Assembly of Terre Haute and Vicinity. All true friends of labor, and those who are in favor of "an honest day's wages for an honest day's work," are respectfully requested to to refuse to patronize those on the list, as they are sustaining with their patronage an institution that in ten years has not paid wages equal to the suport of a family.

Hoberg, Root & Co., Dry Goods, 518 Main.

A. Z. Foster, Carpets, Main Street.

Myers Brothers, Clothiers Fourth and Main.

J. T. H. Miller, Clothing, 522 Main.

P. J. Kaufman, Groceries, Seventh & Main.

W. W. Cliver, Groceries, 631 Main.

Emil Teitge, Pike's Peak Grocery.

A. Eaton, Coal, 723 Main.

A. C. Combs, 122 south Third.

S. C. Stimson, Wall Paper, 673 Main.

J. J. Baur & Son, Druggist, Seventh & Main.

Hall & Mail, Dentists, 529½ Ohio street.

P. J. Ryan, Livery Stable, Second and Main.

X Ed. Roach, Fish Market, Ohio street.

T. J. Griffith, Boots and Shoes, Fourth Street

T. J. Patton, Meat Market, Fourth street.

W. H. Sage, Confectioner, 425 Main.

Hunter's Laundry, 523 Main.

Stein & Heckelsberg, Shoes, 421 Main.

Examples of Knights' tactics: above, a consumer boycott; top right, a general strike; bottom right, worker sabotage.

MARYLAND.—THE LABOR STRIKE IN THE CUMBERLAND REGION—MERCHANTS IN THE MINING TOWN OF FROSTBURG CLOSING THEIR STORES BY ORDER OF THE KNIGHTS OF LABOR.—See Page 267.

THE GREAT STRIKE ON THE SOUTHWESTERN RAILWAY SYSTEM.—"KILLING" AN ENGINE ON THE MISSOURI PACIFIC. SEE PAGE 71.

**Unlike other unions of their era, the Knights actively recruited women. Above, delegates to the 1886 national convention. Below, a survey form used by organizer Leonora Barry.**

tempted to negotiate a settlement. He instructed strikers to return to work and wrote Gould: "The way is clear for settlement in such a way that the relations existing between labor and capital. . .need not experience a jar or shock of any magnitude."

The workers ignored Powderly's efforts and the strike continued until it was broken by force. Although Powderly's assessment of the strike's dismal prospects had been accurate, he had neither the credibility nor structural authority to stop it. The incident revealed a philosophical and practical rift between the rank and file and the national leadership.

One outcome of the strike was cooperation between the Knights and Farmers Alliance members, who supplied food and funds to the striking workers. The Alliance invited the Knights to participate in discussions of independent political action, a notion already popular with the Order's membership. Despite an official ban on direct involvement in electoral politics, hundreds of district and local assemblies created shadow committees to back independent labor candidates in the 1886 elections. They scored impressive upsets in mayoral races, including the ouster of a prominent attorney by a janitor in Waterloo, Iowa.

Although Powderly had been elected mayor of Scranton, Pennsylvania, three times on third party tickets, he resisted the move to create a national third party. Pressure from the rank and file forced a referendum on the subject in 1890. But by the time the People's Party was formally organized two years later, the Order was too feeble to make a significant contribution.

Conflict between the national leadership and the membership arose over other issues, such as Powderly's refusal to support a May 1, 1886 strike for the eight-hour day, the demonstration that established May Day as the international workers holiday. He sent out one of his

**Black delegate Frank Farrell introduces Grand Master Workman Terence Powderly to the 1886 convention.**

"Secret Circulars" with the lame suggestion that Local Assemblies ask members to write short essays on the eight-hour question. Though peaceful, the May Day demonstration by 350,000 workers alarmed employers. Three days later, a bomb exploded at a labor rally in Chicago's Haymarket Square, killing several policemen and triggering a reign of anti-union terror. The use of company spies, blacklisting, injunctions, troops, and red-baiting escalated. While officially disassociated from both events, the Knights suffered from the repressive backlash.

At the same time, the Knights were attacked by rival craft union leaders whose status was threatened by the Order's success in organizing skilled workers. Meeting in Philadelphia, reportedly in silk hats and frock coats, craft union leaders drew up a "treaty of peace" in May 1886 that actually amounted to a call for surrender. The treaty demanded that the Knights relinquish organizing in any trade that had an existing national union. Their ultimatum ignored, the craft unionists consolidated as the American Federation of Labor (AFL), with cigarmaker Samuel Gompers as president.

The Knights were not blameless in the bitter struggle with the craft unions. The Order's position on organizing by trade had been ambivalent; many members belonged both to a craft union and the Knights. By the mid-1880's, such dual loyalties became harder to reconcile. Factions within the Knights exacerbated local jurisdictional battles by refusing to honor craft union labels and organizing

"scabs" who took the place of striking or fired craft unionists at lower pay. They forced craft union members to choose between the Knights and their national unions, and whole assemblies deserted the Order in droves. Although the Knights continued vigorous organizing drives in the rural South and West, by 1890 fewer than 100,000 members remained.

The AFL, meanwhile, grew slowly but steadily. Its appeal was simultaneously more militant and more conservative than the Knights'. Unlike Powderly, Gompers had no reluctance to strike; he scorned the Knights' vision of harmony between capital and labor. But by advancing a brand of "simple unionism" concentrating on "a fair day's wage for a fair day's work," Gompers narrowed the focus of the labor movement. While it paid lipservice to the "ideal of solidarity irrespective of race," the AFL effectively excluded women, minorities, and immigrant laborers by limiting membership to skilled workers. Practicality soon overshadowed principle; rather than challenging the growing concentration of industry, Gompers aligned with powerful industrialists in the National Civic Federation, buying recognition for the elite craft unions at the expense of the unskilled and unorganized majority of workers.

The fight with the AFL, internal schisms, and a series of debilitating conflicts like the Gould strike all contributed to the rapid decline of the Knights. As the 20th century approached the Order faded, but not its vision of a single union for all workers.

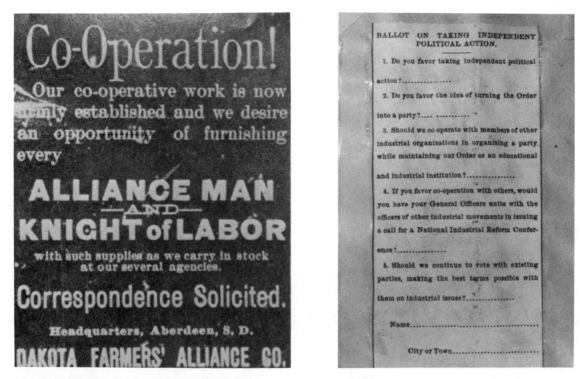

Cooperative enterprises and political action linked the Knights with the Farmers Alliance. Left, an advertisement for a cooperative store. Right, a membership poll.

The cartoonist depicts the disharmony of the labor movement in the late 1880s.

WANTED, A LEADER! — THE LABOR-AGITATION ORCHESTRA ON THE GO-AS-YOU-PLEASE PLAN.

15

# Industrial Unionism: The Story of Steel

The inadequacy of the AFL's craft-union philosophy was especially visible in such mass-production industries as clothing, textiles, grain-milling, meatpacking, and steel. As industrialists mechanized production, historic distinctions between crafts were blurred or erased, key components of the manufacturing process were entrusted to unskilled labor, and the value of craft skills diminished. Professional managers invaded the factory, imposing uniform production standards and supplanting the traditional autonomy of the craft shop.

One outcome of mass production was a decisive advantage for manufacturers in labor conflict. Unskilled workers who walked out could be replaced by strikebreakers without crippling output; community boycotts were ineffectual against products sold in regional or national markets. In the single-company towns which grew up around giant factories, the employer possessed police and judicial powers which could be deployed against protesting workers. Many companies were influential enough to summon further assistance from the federal and state governments for the often brutal task of strikebreaking.

Against such power, workers could muster only sheer numbers and their strategic concentration at a centralized "point of production," the factory floor. Yet it was just this concentration which the craft approach undercut by fragmenting the industrial workforce into innumerable jurisdictions. Labor radicals and rank-and-file activists fashioned an alternative concept of unionism, which emphasized the solidarity of production workers and the value of unified organization. But for nearly half a century the idea of "industrial unionism" was strenuously resisted by trade union officials, who saw it as a challenge to their leadership and a threat to the favored status of their skilled members. Their self-protec-

tive stance left the AFL in a weak position to contest an extended anti-union offensive by American manufacturers. Between the 1880s and the early 1930s, the power of organized labor steadily declined.

Among the mass production industries that blossomed after the Civil War, steel was the flagship: technologically advanced, capital-intensive, and highly concentrated. Through the middle of the 20th century, it retained a sufficiently dominant role in the American economy to merit the popular slogan, "As steel goes so goes the nation."

For labor the slogan was painfully accurate. As aggressive entrepreneurs built and consolidated the steel industry, trade unions maintained a strong position on sufferance from the employers. But beginning with the Homestead conflict in 1892, the steel barons pursued a ruthless policy of wage-cutting and union-busting, which provoked periodic rank-and-file rebellions. Despite the steady erosion of their own position, leaders of the chief steel union failed to exploit these uprisings and sometimes scorned them. Even when the AFL mounted a valiant attempt to organize the industry, a basic ambivalence toward industrial unionism subverted its efforts.

Forty years after Homestead, the steel industry was effectively union-free, as were the newer industries—automobiles, rubber, electrical products—which had followed steel's example in labor policy. Then, very suddenly, a massive upheaval swept through the American workforce. Within a decade, insurgent unions had won recognition from employers in all the mass production industries.

Thus the story of steel is the story of industrial unionism, a tale of repeated failure, wasted opportunities, and periodic heroism, redeemed by a decisive if problematic triumph.

### The Story of Steel

# Homestead

In 1891, the Amalgamated Association of Iron and Steel Workers, an AFL affiliate, was one of the strongest trade unions in the country. Unskilled laborers were not permitted to join but its 24,000 members constituted roughly. two-thirds of the skilled craftsmen in the industry. The Amalgamated had established an elaborate system of wage scales that afforded its members higher pay than most industrial workers.

Andrew Carnegie, the leading steel baron, at first tolerated the union for the stability it provided. Because the Amalgamated set wage levels for the industry, rival producers could not undercut his prices. But once he had eliminated much of the cutthroat competition, Carnegie concentrated on economizing; labor became simply an item of cost, to be kept as low as possible.

As mechanization increased productivity, wage scales were constantly readjusted; union men, paid according to mill output, accepted sharp cuts in their rate of pay per ton. While the Amalgamated was generally accommodating, negotiated wages and working conditions were ultimately unacceptable to management. As one Carnegie partner put it: "The Amalgamated placed a tax on improvements, therefore the Amalgamated had to go."

Carnegie chose his mill in Homestead, Pennsylvania, as the place to do battle. He put the mill under the charge of Henry Clay Frick, already notorious for smashing union organizing in the coal fields. With the Amalgamated contract coming up for renewal in 1892, Frick delivered an ultimatum to Homestead workers: if they did not accept another severe wage cut by June 24, he would no longer recognize the union.

The Amalgamated offered a compromise, expecting further negotiations, but Frick had already erected a 15-foot fence around the perimeter of the mill, topped with barbed wire and pierced with holes for guns. Unbeknownst to the union, Frick had also made inquiries about hiring a private army from the Pinkerton Company, a detective agency that provided security to manufacturers during strikes and lockouts.

Frick never intended to negotiate. He let the deadline pass and then shut down sections of the mill, firing hundreds of workers and forcing the union to strike. Though only one-fourth of the 4000 Homestead workers belonged to the union, the unskilled majority joined forces with the Amalgamated and refused to work. By July 2, the mill was idle and the company announced to the press that, "hereafter the Homestead steel works will be operated as a non-union mill."

WORKMEN CANNONADING THE BARGES.

SOLDIERS IN CAMP.

WORKMEN ATTACKING THE BARGES.

SURRENDER OF THE PINKERTON MEN.

GREAT BATTLE OF HOMESTEAD.
Defeat and Capture of the
PINKERTON INVADERS
July 6th 1892.

PINKERTON'S CAPTIVES ON THEIR WAY TO PRISON.

16

The union appointed a 50-member Advisory Committee which took control of the town, shutting the saloons and keeping the peace. Under the leadership of Hugh O'Donnell, the strikers established round-the-clock picket lines and manned outposts to watch for strikebreakers.

The Pinkertons arrived a few days later. Some 300 armed agents attempted to enter the mill secretly by a river landing, but union scouts spotted their barges. Hundreds of workers met them at the landing at four in the morning.

Someone fired a shot, from which side is unknown, and the Pinkerton captain gave the order to fire. In the ensuing volley, seven workers and four Pinkertons were killed. The battle continued throughout the day with workers bombarding the barges with cannon fire, explosives, and burning oil. Finally, the Pinkertons surrendered and were hastily expelled from town.

Asserting that the strikers had violated property rights by preventing the company from taking lawful possession of the mill, Frick appealed to the governor to send the militia. The town sheriff, whose authority had been usurped by the Advisory Committee, made the same request. Because there had been no further violence after the battle at the landing, the strikers assumed the soldiers would be neutral at worst; they planned a welcoming ceremony complete with brass bands. The workers even debated which song would be appropriate, rejecting "When Johnny Comes Marching Home" and "Hold the Fort" in favor of the more festive "Ta Ra Ra Boom De Ay."

The bands never played because the 6000 troops took Homestead by surprise in the early morning hours. Their commanding officer rejected O'Donnell's overtures and soon soldiers were escorting strikebreakers into the mill. Frick added legal intimidation to his strikebreaking tactics. In fact, both sides pressed charges stemming from the battle at the landing though company officials were spared the humiliation of being hauled to jail while the union struggled to pay a flood of bail bonds. In all, strike leaders faced 167 indictments on charges including murder and treason.

For five months, the union distributed relief supplies and conducted weekly rallies. Flyers dropped into the millyards urged scabs to leave and some did, with their fares home paid by the Amalgamated. Around the country, unionists rallied to the cause. Several Carnegie mills were shut down by sympathy strikes and picketers at labor recruitment agencies in New York tried to stop the flow of strikebreakers. In Pittsburgh, union members demanded that the city reject a Carnegie gift of one million dollars for a new library.

The AFL considered a secondary boycott of Carnegie products but instead declared December 13 "Homestead Day" to raise funds for the strikers. The federation's support was too little, too late. With 2000 strikebreakers at work, the mill was back in operation. Seeing little chance of victory, many of the unskilled workers threatened to defect. On November 21, the Amalgamated called off the strike.

The results were lower wages, longer hours, and the crippling of the Amalgamated. Nearly 2500 Homestead workers lost their mill jobs permanently. As Carnegie applied the Homestead labor policy to other mills and competing steelmakers followed his lead, the union's membership dropped in two years from 24,000 to 10,000. The Amalgamated ignored the warning implicit in the Homestead conflict. Its strength had been based on its ability to withhold skilled labor, but Frick had proven that with new technology he could reopen the mill with inexperienced workers who were outside the traditional purview of craft unionism. By continuing to exclude unskilled workers, the Amalgamated became an accomplice to its own demise.

**State militia enter Homestead, PA.**

## *The Story of Steel*
# The Wobblies

In 1901, Andrew Carnegie and other major steel producers joined forces with Wall Street financiers to create the United States Steel Corporation, a giant trust controlling 60 percent of the industry. Perceiving this consolidation as a threat, the Amalgamated launched a calamitous strike which ended with the union losing its contracts in 15 mills and agreeing to abandon organizing efforts in all non-union plants.

With the union suppressed, the financiers who dominated the new trust instituted a more conciliatory approach to labor relations. Judge Elbert H. Gary, chief executive officer, urged plant managers to "take care of your men," to foster "a community of interest between proprietors and wage earners." U.S. Steel affiliates constructed low-rent housing and offered employees low-interest home loans, disability benefits, and a discount stock purchase plan. Most mill towns had an elaborate Carnegie library containing a music hall and swimming pool. The steel trust made substantial contributions to churches and organizations like the YMCA.

The conspicuous paternalism of the steel trust had little effect on the harsh reality of life in the mill towns. Above, a Carnegie library and gymnasium. Below, scenes of Homestead, a U.S. Steel town.

Few workers had enough money to buy homes or stock, even at discount rates; these programs were targeted to a thin layer of skilled workers, whom the company courted at the same time it was suffocating their union. Most men, compelled to work 12-hour shifts and seven-day weeks, had little opportunity to enjoy libraries, concerts or Sunday chapel. But the company's largesse influenced the merchant and professional classes in the mill towns who came to share not only the same clubs, schools, and churches as company officials but the same outlook. Reliant on corporate philanthropy, community institutions which otherwise might have been neutral or sympathetic to the workers tended to identify with the employer's interests.

The paternalistic strategy articulated by Judge Gary solidified company control over the mill communities, defused public criticism, and built a base of support among elite elements of the workforce. All this would serve the industry well in the labor battles to come. But his programs did little to improve the lives of most steelworkers. Underneath the veneer of paternalism, conditions remained harsh in the mill towns.

McKees Rocks, Pennsylvania, was the site of a railroad car plant owned by a U.S. Steel subsidiary, the Pressed Steel Car Company. The "company houses" were shacks without water or toilets. Rents were high, workers were required to patronize stores owned by company agents, and plant superintendents routinely extorted payments in exchange for jobs.

Sixteen nationalities were represented among the 5000 steelworkers at the McKees Rocks plant. Like other steel companies, Pressed Steel Car deliberately pitted ethnic groups against each other in the hope of impeding

labor solidarity. Skilled positions were generally reserved for American-born workers. With access to a seemingly inexhaustible supply of immigrant laborers, the company felt immune to wage demands. President Frank N. Hoffstot was candid about the policy: "We buy labor in the cheapest market," he told reporters.

Between 1907 and 1909, wages at McKees Rocks were cut drastically; workers who had been earning three to five dollars a day in 1907 were taking home 50 cents to a dollar two years later. During the same period, the company introduced assembly lines which intensified the pace of production and a system of "pooled" wages which penalized employees for any delay in the production process, regardless of cause. Since the rates were not posted, workers had no way to calculate their earnings. Sometimes, when a "pool" failed to meet its production quota, its members went unpaid.

On July 12, 1909, forty immigrant riveters refused to work until wage rates were posted, pooling was abolished, and wages were restored to pre-1907 levels. Within three days the entire plant was shut down as skilled, American-born workers, nursing grievances of their own, closed ranks with the unskilled.

The company moved quickly to break the strike, calling in scabs, armed deputies, and mounted state troopers whom the workers referred to as "the Cossacks." In an incident reminiscent of Homestead, the strikers repelled a steamboat bringing scabs to the mill. When 50 mounted troopers tried to evict striking workers from company houses, the wives threatened to burn the shacks and shouted: "Kill the Cossacks! . . . Stamp them out! If you are afraid, go home to the children and leave the work to us." A battle ensued and the evictions were halted.

With no established labor organizations in the plant, the strike's leadership was improvised. Soon after the walkout, the strikers empowered a committee known as "the Big Six" to negotiate with the company. The Big Six was dominated by skilled workers who wanted to end the strike as quickly as possible, on terms unacceptable to the

**IWW members picket during a strike against the Oliver Steel Company, Pittsburgh, PA.**

23

unskilled majority. As the split in the ranks became evident, leadership devolved to the "Unknown Committee," a network of foreign-born workers, some with experience in European labor movements. The Unknown Committee organized elaborate sentry systems and 24-hour picketing to repel strikebreakers and maintain morale among the strikers.

During the first month of the walkout another organization entered the picture—the Industrial Workers of the World (IWW), a new national industrial union with a militant reputation. IWW organizers came to McKees Rocks as advisors to the Unknown Committee and gradually assumed a more prominent role. In mid-August, IWW orators addressed a mass meeting of workers in six languages and hammered on the theme of industrial unionism. Soon after, the strikers announced that "inspired by the principles of class solidarity" they had organized the Car Builders International Union, IWW. National publicity generated by the IWW stirred public sympathy for the workers and attracted contributions to the strike fund.

By early September, pressures for a settlement were mounting on both sides. A federal investigator had been dispatched to McKees Rocks and influential figures in Pittsburgh decried company intransigence for giving the radical IWW a foothold. On the other side, the strikers' initial success in repelling strikebreakers proved difficult to sustain and the skilled workers were on the verge of defection.

The resulting agreement was widely hailed as a victory for the workers, although the actual terms of settlement were less favorable than they first appeared. Regardless of the result, unskilled steelworkers—immigrants from more than a dozen nations—had proved that they could organize in a disciplined and militant fashion. They had done so despite friction with the skilled workers and a disavowal from the AFL, whose Secretary-Treasurer, Frank Morrison, blamed the strike on "ignorant foreign labor, aliens who do not speak our language or understand our institutions."

The implications were clear to Amalgamated leader P.J. McArdle, who wrote to Morrison: "There is no question but that more and more of the foreign born workers in the industry are becoming impressed by the vision held out by the Industrial Unionists, and the victory at McKees Rocks has given them a strong talking point—so much so, in fact, that even our members are beginning to pay attention to what they say."

It was the AFL's failure to organize the "entire working class"—including the foreign-born, the unskilled, migrants, blacks, Asians, and women—which had led to the creation of the IWW in 1905. In many respects, the IWW began where the Knights of Labor left off. Membership was open to all wage earners. IWW members, or "Wobblies" as they called themselves, stressed the need for "one big union" to match the consolidation of modern industry. Like the Knights, the Wobblies envisioned "a

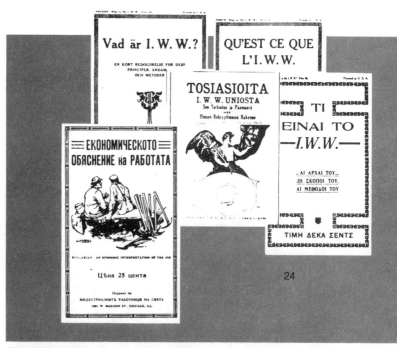

The IWW's outreach to immigrant laborers was a sharp contrast to the chauvinism of the AFL.

new society within the shell of the old," in which the antagonism between capital and labor would be abolished.

But while the Knights were committed to social reform, the Wobbly spirit was revolutionary. The IWW saw industrial society as an unremitting class struggle, and its constitution bluntly declared: "The working class and the employing class have nothing in common." Its ultimate goal was the abolition of capital and the seizure of industry by the workers.

This uncompromising doctrine represented a fusion of ideology and experience. Marxian socialism had taken root in the United States during the previous decade. For many American radicals, Marx's rigorous analysis of class conflict had superceded the utopian ideals which inspired the Knights, the Populists, and other 19th century movements.

In the same era, mine companies in the Rocky Mountain states were using private armies, state troops, legislation, and the courts to break the considerable power of the Western Federation of Miners. In the mining towns, class war was not just a theory, but a harsh reality, and it generated an indigenous brand of militant industrial unionism.

When these dissident western unionists joined forces with Socialist Party activists and freelance radicals, the product was the IWW. The founding convention in Chicago on June 27, 1905, attracted over 200 delegates from 34 organizations; the labor delegates represented 60,000 workers ready to join. But the shared commitment to industrial unionism and revolutionary class struggle masked deep divisions among the founders. The most divisive issue was the role of political action.

Socialists saw unionism as a vehicle for building a mass base for socialism within the working classes; their

**The IWW placed action before theory, disparaging the electoral strategy of the Socialists and the ideological preoccupation of other radicals.**

primary goal was to capture the state. But IWW unionists like Vincent St. John ridiculed the electoral process and viewed government, in St. John's words, as "a committee to look after the interests of the employers."

Veterans of the Western Federation of Miners had seen the entire apparatus of government deployed against them. They believed that progressive reforms enacted by legislation could only be enforced by the direct action of workers "at the point of production"—the mine, the mill, the factory. And they recognized that much of the IWW constituency, including blacks, women, aliens, and migrants, could not vote.

The issue was resolved in 1908, when delegates to the national convention deposed the Socialist faction and excised all references to electoral politics from the IWW constitution. The convention committed the union entirely to direct action.

The most common form of action was the strike; for the Wobblies, strikes not only served to win immediate gains in wages and working conditions, but to "raise the consciousness and aggressiveness of the working class." As one IWW pamphlet phrased it, "We learn to fight by fighting." While other unions struck to win contracts, the Wobblies refused to sign agreements with employers which ceded the right to strike "when you like and wherever you like." Short, intermittent work stoppages kept employers off balance and eased the burden of providing relief funds to strikers. Moreover, a contract might commit workers to remain on the job while fellow workers in a related plant or industry went out on strike.

The IWW devised creative direct action tactics, including the first recorded sit-down strike in the U.S.; after three Wobblies were fired in December 1906, 3000 workers refused to leave a General Electric factory in Schenectady, New York. During a series of "Free Speech" fights in the Pacific Northwest, hundreds of Wobblies defied bans against streetcorner speaking, mounting the soapbox one after another to invite arrest. By filling the jails beyond capacity, they forced town officials to repeal the restrictive laws.

## SABOTAGE

The black cat and wooden shoe—known as "sabot" in French—were the visual symbols of sabotage, the most controversial IWW tactic. While popularly equated with violent destruction of property, the Wobbly definition encompassed an array of non-violent, on-the-job actions.

**"Sabotage means either to slacken up and intefere with the quantity or to botch in your skill and intefere with the quality of capitalist production so as to give poor service. It is something that is fought out within the walls of the shop. Sabotage is not physical violence; sabotage is an internal industrial process."**

Elizabeth Gurley Flynn
IWW organizer

26

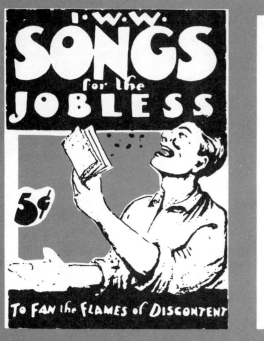

27

Despite a tendency toward hit-and-run organizing, the IWW established a stable presence in some Western communities.

New York City headquarters after a government raid

With their militant tactics and ideology, the Wobblies made inroads among Western loggers, miners, and migrant harvesters. Between 1909 and 1913 they launched a number of forays into the Eastern mass production industries demonstrating—as at McKees Rocks—the potential for organizing unskilled, immigrant workers. Yet, despite some heady victories, such as the 1912 strike by 22,000 textile workers in Lawrence, Massachusetts, the IWW failed to build a stable mass organization. One year after the Lawrence strike, fewer than 700 IWW members remained in the mills; one year after McKees Rocks, the Car Builders International Union was defunct.

Intense employer opposition and government repression were partly responsible for the transiency of the IWW, but Wobbly organizing methods were also at fault. The pattern at McKees Rocks was typical of Eastern drives, where IWW organizers generally intervened as a strike was in progress and moved on once a settlement was reached. There weren't enough organizers to do more. In keeping with its commitment to organize the unorganized, IWW dues and initiation fees were extremely low, and the union could not afford to pay salaries. Not many organizers could be recruited on that basis.

A zealous commitment to democracy contributed to organizational instability; some IWW locals in the West rotated officers every week. And the IWW's no contract policy offered union members scant protection from reprisal. Once the fervor of strike action had subsided, employers could easily purge Wobblies from the payroll.

At its tenth anniversary, the IWW claimed only 15,000 members, a figure that was probably inflated. But an economic boom generated by World War I and a new approach to organizing migrant harvesters produced sudden gains. Wobbly organizers known as "job delegates" obtained work in the fields and drew pay while organizing

Hostile cartoonists pictured the Wobblies as tools of the German enemy.

**Nearly 1200 striking miners are loaded in cattle cars at Bisbee, Arizona, July 1917. Deported to New Mexico, they were imprisoned for two months in an army stockade.**

on the job. While revolutionary goals were not abandoned, the new Agricultural Workers Organization moderated its demands, avoided precipitous strikes, and built a solid union which secured higher wages, shorter hours, and better living conditions for the migrants.

Membership doubled between 1916 and 1917, approaching 100,000. On the eve of U.S. intervention in the war, Wobbly staffer Ben Williams could note with satisfaction that, "The IWW is passing out of the purely propaganda stage and is entering the stage of constructive organization."

But the war cut short the life of the organization. The IWW publicly opposed U.S. intervention, advising men "to fight on the job for yourself and your class" and did not flinch at calling strikes in the vital copper and lumber industries. These actions provided a rationale for a government drive to eradicate the Wobbly "menace." On September 5, 1917, federal agents launched a simultaneous raid against IWW headquarters, local halls, and members' homes. Hundreds of first- and second-line leaders were sentenced to prison terms of up to 20 years.

Defending imprisoned leaders diverted the IWW from organizing and allowed internal conflicts to fester. By the time the nation returned to peacetime "normalcy" and some Wobbly leaders emerged from prison, the union was too debilitated to recover. When the vision of industrial unionism was finally realized, the revolutionary connotations the IWW attached to it had been lost.

**The struggle to free jailed leaders consumed the IWW after World War I.**

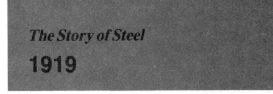

# The Story of Steel
## 1919

In 1909, U.S. Steel dismissed the Amalgamated's residual claims to recognition, posting an "open shop" declaration which abolished negotiated wage scales. Because of its leading position in American industry, unionists considered the Steel Corporation's announcement a threat to all of organized labor. The Amalgamated and the AFL acknowledged the imperative to organize unskilled workers if collective bargaining was to be restored. But although the AFL made steel its primary target, its efforts remained feeble until organizing prospects improved with the advent of World War I.

The war brought increased demand for steel and severe labor shortages. Capitalizing on the situation, the Amalgamated organized 35 new lodges and grew to 15,000 members by the end of the first year of U.S. involvement in the war. The most important boost to organizing, though, was the federal government's changing role in labor relations.

Fearing that labor disturbances would confound the war effort, President Woodrow Wilson established a War Labor Conference Board to ensure uninterrupted production. He actively solicited the AFL's cooperation. In return, the Board asserted "the right of workers to organize in trade unions" and began intervening in workplace disputes on the side of labor. In 1918, the Board delivered a stunning victory to Chicago packinghouse workers, ordering an eight-hour day with ten hours pay and additional pay increases. William Z. Foster, one of the packinghouse organizers and a former Wobbly, was so en-

couraged by this success in a mass production industry that he proposed an industry-wide organizing drive in steel.

Following approval of Foster's proposal at the June 1918 AFL convention, 24 craft unions with members in the steel plants formed the National Committee to Organize Iron and Steel Workers. Foster was designated Secretary-Treasurer and chief tactician.

The self-interests of the participating unions prevented a true industrial union approach. New members recruited through the organizing drive signed a standard application and were then assigned to appropriate trade jurisdictions. Locals of the various unions formed central labor bodies in each district to coordinate efforts but these inter-trade councils were granted no real decision-making powers. Though the Amalgamated would be assigned roughly half of all new members, like the other participants, it pledged only $100 and one organizer to the drive.

With insufficient resources to begin a national campaign, the strategy was to begin organizing in peripheral regions and work towards the industry stronghold in Pittsburgh. The drive commenced in the Chicago district in August 1918 and initial results were astonishing: 1200 signed up in one day in Joliet, 1500 in South Chicago.

The National Committee took advantage of wartime propaganda, equating union membership with other patriotic commitments. Organizers told the workers it was their duty to buy Liberty bonds, increase production, and join the union. "If the world is to be made safe for democracy, there must be economic democracy with political democracy," proclaimed *The American Federationist*, the AFL newspaper.

Aside from these rhetorical appeals, wages and

**President Wilson's intervention transformed the character of labor relations during World War I.**

**A steelworkers rally in Gary, IN.**

33

working conditions provided ample reason for the steelworkers' enthusiastic response to the union. Half of all U.S. Steel employees worked 12-hour days, and half of those labored seven days a week. The average earnings of 72 percent of the workers were below the federal government's "minimum comfort" level and a third earned less than the "minimum subsistence" standard.

The wartime threat of nationalization constrained the industry's reaction. But once armistice was declared in November 1918, employer resistance mounted. The steel trust commissioned hundreds of company spies and routinely discharged workers for union activity. Vowing never to negotiate, Judge Gary declared that if the workers wanted a voice, "let them buy stock."

By the spring of 1919, the National Committee had recruited 100,000 members and organizing began in the Pittsburgh district. As expected, the unions' entrance into Pittsburgh met the stiffest repression yet. Local officials denied outdoor meeting permits and landlords refused to rent meeting halls. One sympathetic landlord in Rankin who defied anti-union sentiment saw his building closed by the Board of Health. The mayor of Duquesne pronounced that, "Jesus Christ himself could not speak in Duquesne for the AF of L." "Flying squadrons" of organizers launched free speech fights reminiscent of the Wobblies; they staged mass marches with uniformed ex-servicemen in the lead, forcing local officials to acquiesce.

The Pittsburgh drive was taking hold but, as one organizer put it, "the dam broke before the district was more than half worked." Union members grew impatient at unkept wartime promises and threatened to strike. With less than 20 percent of the industry organized, the National Committee did not believe a strike could succeed but it bowed to rank and file pressure to hold a vote. When the ballots were counted, 98 percent had voted to walk out if basic demands for higher wages, shorter hours, better conditions, and union recognition were not met.

Still reluctant to call a strike, the National Committee attempted to negotiate with Judge Gary and asked President Wilson to intercede. When Gary dismissed even his appeal, Wilson requested a postponement of union action. But the rank and file were determined; the strike began September 22, and a week later the National Committee claimed that over 350,000 workers had left the mills.

The steel companies retaliated on two fronts, in the milltowns and the media. Pittsburgh district authorities again suppressed civil liberties. Sheriff W.S. Haddock outlawed outdoor meetings in Allegheny County and deputized 5000 company men. Police in McKeesport forbade more than six strikers to convene anywhere, including their own headquarters. State troopers wielded clubs at peaceful gatherings, dragged strikers from their homes, and jailed hundreds on trumped up charges. The strike was relatively peaceful in other districts except for Gary, Indiana, where federal troops were called in after a police-incited riot.

The companies also launched a massive propaganda effort, exploiting the post-war "Red Scare" mentality. A series of 30 full-page ads in the Pittsburgh newspapers contended that "the steel strike can't win. It is uncalled for and un-American. It is led by men who apparently are trying to establish the 'red' rule of anarchy and bolshevism in this land of opportunity and liberty. Be a 100% American. . . Go back to work."

The strike's strength among Slavic immigrants bolstered the chauvinistic attacks, and Foster's Wobbly background lent some credence to the claims that the

34

"When our organization would meet employers, the barrier that was held up before them was, 'Why don't you go to the steel mills? You get the steel mill conditions up, get the hours down, and the wages up there, and when you do that, of course, we will treat with you then.' And that was the one situation that made it absolutely imperative that the steel mills be organized, because it held the balance of the labor movement back."

John Fitzpatrick
Chairman of the National Committee

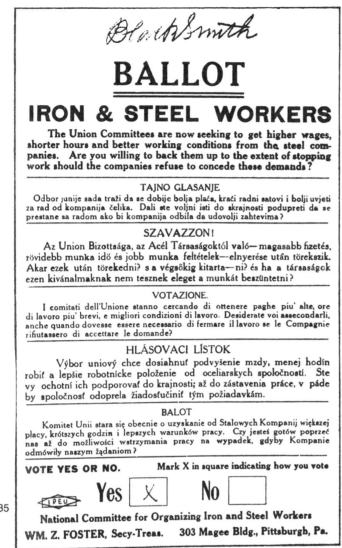

*Blacksmith*

# BALLOT

## IRON & STEEL WORKERS

The Union Committees are now seeking to get higher wages, shorter hours and better working conditions from the steel companies. Are you willing to back them up to the extent of stopping work should the companies refuse to concede these demands?

### TAJNO GLASANJE

Odbor junije sada traži da se dobije bolja plaća, kraći radni satovi i bolji uvjeti za rad od kompanija čelika. Dali ste voljni isti do skrajnosti podupreti da se prestane sa radom ako bi kompanija odbila da udovolji zahtevima?

### SZAVAZZON!

Az Union Bizottsága, az Acél Társaságoktól való— magasabb fizetés, rövidebb munka idö és jobb munka feltételek—elnyerése után törekszik. Akar ezek után törekedni? s a végsökig kitarta—ni? és ha a társaságok ezen kivánalmaknak nem tesznek eleget a munkát beszüntetni?

### VOTAZIONE.

I comitati dell'Unione stanno cercando di ottenere paghe piu' alte, ore di lavoro piu' brevi, e migliori condizioni di lavoro. Desiderate voi assecondarli, anche quando dovesse essere necessario di fermare il lavoro se le Compagnie rifiutassero di accettare le domande?

### HLÁSOVACI LÍSTOK

Výbor uniový chce dosiahnuť podvyšenie mzdy, menej hodín robiť a lepšie robotnícke položenie od oceliarskych spoločností. Ste vy ochotní ich podporovať do krajnosti; až do zástavenia práce, v páde by spoločnosť odoprela žiadosťučiniť tým požiadavkám.

### BALLOT

Komitet Unii stara się obecnie o uzyskanie od Stalowych Kompanij większej płacy, krótszych godzin i lepszych warunków pracy. Czy jesteś gotów poprzeć nas aż do możliwości wstrzymania pracy na wypadek, gdyby Kompanie odmówiły naszym żądaniom?

**VOTE YES OR NO.**    Mark X in square indicating how you vote

Yes [ X ]    No [ ]

**National Committee for Organizing Iron and Steel Workers**
**WM. Z. FOSTER, Secy.-Treas.**    303 Magee Bldg., Pittsburgh, Pa.

35

union leadership was "red." With the war over, the federal government no longer had an incentive to intervene, and the industry's success in portraying the strike as a dangerous, radical movement undercut political support for the strikers.

With the tide of public opinion rising against it, the strike was also beset with internal problems. One strike leader lamented, "this organization has as much cohesiveness as a load of furniture." The Amalgamated's participation was, at best, half-hearted. It derived great benefit from the organizing drive, tripling its cash reserves between 1918 and 1920, but contributed little, expending less than half of its own special strike fund. A substantial portion of the National Committee's relatively meager strike funds actually came from unions outside the industry, notably the Amalgamated Clothing Workers and the International Ladies Garment Workers. Constant jurisdictional squabbling undermined solidarity and the National Committee had no authority to hold the individual unions accountable.

Intent on demoralizing and dividing the strike force, company spies and the press spread reports of strikers returning to work and production resuming normal levels. Newspaper accounts claimed almost ten times as many returned workers as there were jobs in the industry. The Amalgamated contributed to the defections, ordering 5000 of its members under contract with independent mills to go back to work. Employers augmented their depleted workforce by importing 30,000 black strikebreakers. These new recruits felt little reason to honor the strike because the unions had excluded the several thousand blacks who came to the mills during the war years.

By mid-December, the number of strikers had dwin-

**Women on picket duty raise relief funds for striking workers.**

36

dled to 109,000. The National Committee conceded on January 8, 1920, calling off the strike "pending preparations for the next big organization movement." The Amalgamated foreclosed the possibility of reorganization; it withdrew from the National Committee and squandered the funds it derived from the campaign on a plush new headquarters.

The Interchurch World Movement, a federation of Protestant denominations which investigated the strike and attempted to mediate it, concluded: "The United States Steel Corporation was too big to be beaten by 300,000 working men. It had too large a cash surplus, too many allies among other businesses, too much support from government officers, local and national, too strong influence with social institutions such as the press and the pulpit, it spread over too much of the earth—still retaining absolutely centralized control—to be defeated by widely scattered workers of many minds, many fears, varying states of pocketbook and under a comparatively improvised leadership."

The steel strike was the highlight of a turbulent year in labor relations; one out of five employed workers in the United States was on strike in 1919, a higher proportion than in any year before or since. Though the strike failed completely, the report of the Interchurch World Movement sparked a controversy that helped to make working hours, collective bargaining, and the civil liberties of workers more urgent public issues. By 1923, the 12-hour day had been abolished in the steel industry. Collective bargaining made less progress, and the labor movement lost ground in the 1920s. But the 1919 strike had taught some AFL leaders a bitter lesson about the frailty of craft union coalitions.

Company propaganda helped undermine the strike.

Federal troops stationed in Gary.

## The Story of Steel
# The Rank and File and the CIO

After the failure of the great 1919 strikes, the labor movement entered a period of severe decline. The AFL lost a million members between 1920 and 1923. In the steel industry, the Amalgamated Association survived the '20s as a tiny business organization for highly skilled workers in a few antiquated mills. Amalgamated president Michael Tighe was derisively known throughout the labor movement as "Grandmother."

When the Depression hit in the 1930s, steel was the exemplar of a non-union industry. Wages for common labor ranked 20th among 21 major industries. A decade later all the major steel producers had been unionized, steel labor enjoyed one of the highest hourly wages in American industry, and a national union of steel workers claimed 660,000 members. How did this sudden turnabout occur?

Repeating an historic pattern, the initial effect of the Depression was to increase unemployment and demoralize labor; there was little protest at first. But the collapse was so deep, widespread, and long-lasting that it undermined popular faith in the nation's political and economic system. Americans expressed their disaffection at the polls, electing politicans at all levels who were less accommodating to corporate leaders. The shift in federal posture under President Franklin D. Roosevelt was especially telling. Administration policies displayed an inconsistent but marked tilt toward labor, which at once reflected and stimulated the massive grassroots organizing campaign which galvanized the steel mills in the 1930s.

The initial catalyst was the passage of the National Industrial Recovery Act in 1933. This emergency measure allowed manufacturers collaborating under government supervision to fix prices and set production quotas. To balance this major concession to industry, labor received certain protections. The most important was a provision, section 7(a), which promised workers "the right to organize and bargain collectively through representatives of their own choosing," without "inteference, restraint, or coercion from employers."

Although the AFL did little initially to publicize the new law, workers who heard of 7(a) rushed to join unions. Two hundred locals with 100,000 members appeared in the auto industry; 385,000 textile workers were unionized; 90,000 steel workers applied to join the Amalgamated.

But many craft union leaders did not welcome the industrial masses clamoring at their doorsteps. George Patterson, a rank and file organizer from Chicago, recalls: "I got in touch with the Amalgamated Association. . . and

**The surge of unionism in 1933 brought industrial conflict to the steel mills. Left, armed deputies attack a crowd of pickets at a Pittsburgh plant. Right, a circular issued by rank and file leaders urges workers to boycott a company union election.**

## WORKERS DO NOT BE MISLED

Do not vote at election the company will hold Monday, December 11th. The United States National Labor Board will hold the only election to decide who shall represent you. If you vote Monday you will vote for the Cmpany Union. Do not vote until Government Officials take charge.

### ROBOTNÍCI NEDAJTE SA PODVIEŠŤ.

Nehlasujte na voľbu vydržiavanú KOMPANIOU, ktorá bude v pondelok 11-ho decembra 1933, až keď The United States National Labor Board bude vydržiavať schôdzu, ktorá rozrieši, kto má vás zastupovať.

Keď budete voliť, v pondelok, budete voliť za Kompanicku Uniu. Nevoľte až keď Vládny Úrad nariadi voľbu.

'Εργάται μὴ σᾶς γελάσουν. Μὴ ψηφίσετε εἰς τὰς ἐκλογὰς τῆς 'Εταιρείας, τὴν Δευτέραν 11ην Δεχεμβρίου τῶν 'Ηνωμένων Πολιτειῶν 'Εργατικὸν Συμγούλιον θὰ προβῆ εἰς τὴν ἐκλογὴν νὰ ἀποφανθῆ ποῖος θὰ σᾶς ἀντιπροσωπεύση. 'Εὰν ψηφίσητε τὴν Δευτέραν θὰ ψηφίσητε τῆς 'Εταιρείας Σύνδεσμον. Μὴ ψηφίσητε μέχρι ἡ Διεύθυνσις τῆς Κυβερνήσεως ἀναλάβει τὴν ἐκλογήν.

Weir-Cove Lodge, No. 30, W. Va.—Wm. Long, President.
Valley Lodge, No. 31, W. Va.—Mel Moore, President.
Blue Eagle Lodge, No. 32, W. Va.—Thomas Murray, President.
New Deal Lodge, No. 33, W. Va.—Charles Green, wood, President.
NRA Lodge, No. 35, W. Va.—Chas. Anderson, President.
Progressive Lodge, No. 38, W. Va.—Henry Fisher, President.
Good Will Lodge, No. 39, W. Va.—Jacob Entinger, President
Steubenville Lodge, No. 150, Ohio—George Dunn, President.

**AMALGAMATED ASSOCIATION OF IRON, STEEL AND TIN WORKERS OF NORTH AMERICA.**

40

they wouldn't have anything to do with us. . . (They) wrote me nice letters, but never came to see me or invited me to come down or talk over joining with them. The Amalgamated was just lying there and wouldn't do a thing for us."

Conflict erupted immediately between the new unionists and the Amalgamated's old guard. When 10,000 workers struck a mill in Wierton, West Virginia, in October 1933, Tighe condemned the walkout. The newly created National Labor Board intervened and the strikers returned to work in anticipation of a promised election. Once production resumed, however, the company double-crossed the union by leaving it off the ballot.

Disgusted with Tighe, activists from 50 local steel workers lodges joined forces in a "Rank and File Movement." Among its leaders were William J. Long, president of the Wierton Lodge, and Earl Forbeck, a subforeman in McKeesport who had organized 30 new lodges with 18,000 members. The rank and filers took control of the Amalgamated's 1934 convention and approved Forbeck's proposal for an industry-wide strike in June unless the steel companies recognized the union.

When, as expected, the companies refused to confer with the Amalgamated, the rank and filers demanded the use of union headquarters and $10,000 in union funds to conduct the strike. Tighe refused. Fearing that a strike was likely to fail, the dissidents appealed to President Roosevelt. He offered government-supervised elections, a proposal dismissed as "bunk" in light of the Wierton experience. This widened the split with Tighe, who labeled the rank and filers "Communist and vipers."

While employers stockpiled guns and ammunition and girded for the strike, the government made a final offer—a special Steel Board to hear the workers' grievances. Again, the rank and filers were unimpressed, calling the deal the "National Run Around," but their weak position compelled them to accept the offer and call off the strike.

In the meantime, United Mine Workers president John L. Lewis and other proponents of industrial unionism were pressing their case within the AFL, making steel the centerpiece of their argument. In his report to the 1934 AFL convention, Tighe admitted that the Amalgamated had not converted the flood of rank and file activists into dues-paying members. From Lewis' perspective, this was indefensible. Steel was the bulwark of anti-unionism; if it were organized other industries would follow. Lewis had a more direct interest as well; some of his members worked in "captive mines" owned by the steel companies and their bargaining position was handicapped by the low wage levels in steel.

The 1934 convention ultimately approved a compromise resolution, shaped by Lewis, which upheld the jurisdictional rights of the craft unions while asserting the need to organize "on a different basis" in the mass production industries. The resolution explicitly called for a campaign in iron and steel, but continued bickering between

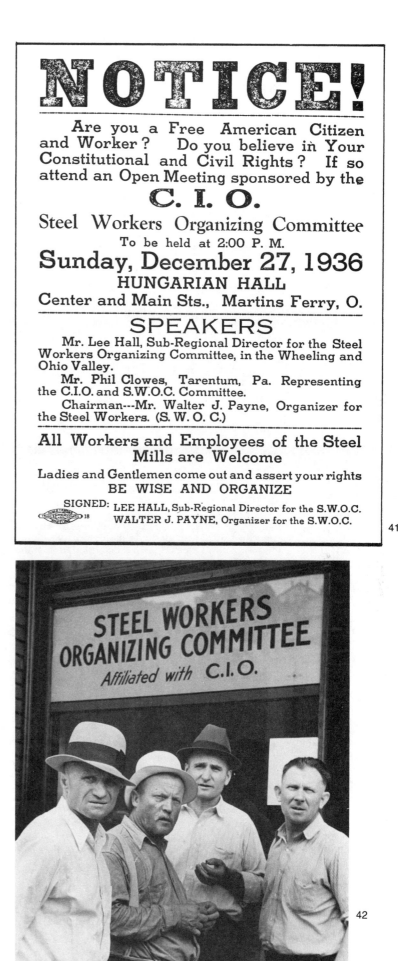

41

42

Rank and file activists used their positions as elected employee "reps" to undermine the company unions. At the Pittsburgh meeting, 250 reps affiliated with the CIO steel drive.

Tighe and the Rank and File Movement stalled its implementation. When the rank and filers defied Tighe and held their own conferences, he expelled 75 percent of the membership. Although AFL president William Green managed to patch up the split, the steel campaign had still not begun by the time the 1935 AFL convention opened in Atlantic City.

The situation in steel was hardly unique. Bewildered by the conduct of union leaders, and disappointed by the failure of the government to enforce section 7(a), workers in all the mass production industries were deserting the unions as abruptly as they had joined. The stage was set for a showdown and this time the chasm between craft and industrial unionism was too great to bridge with a compromise. The day after the convention, Lewis called a meeting of his allies from the Mineworkers, Typographers, and the garment industry unions. A few weeks later, they formed the Committee for Industrial Organizing (CIO).

Despite declarations of fealty to the Federation, Green and other craft union leaders perceived the CIO as an enormous threat and urged it to disband. Steel continued to be a focus of contention. Lewis offered Green $500,000 for a steel drive if the AFL would contribute $1 million and agree to organize along industrial lines. Green countered by soliciting support for an AFL-sponsored campaign, but of the 110 member unions canvassed for contributions, only 38 replied and only five submitted pledges totalling $8,625.

Lewis made a similar offer to Tighe, pointedly including a provision that the campaign be conducted by "competent leadership." Backed by pressure from the rank and filers in the mills, Lewis' offer hardened to an

"I remember those mornings in the spring of 1937 . . . There would be about six organizers from the union and six volunteers. We broke open the bundles of *Steel Labor*, inserted the leaflets and retied them with twine, placed the bundles in the trunks of the cars and off we'd go to the plant gates to catch the day shift going in . . . Most would smile and take the literature. A few would look angry or cuss and say, 'Keep it, we don't need you,' but most of the fellows were eager for it and would holler, 'Good work, boys!'"

Mario Manzardo
CIO organizer

ultimatum and Tighe succumbed. On June 4, 1936, the Amalgamated joined the CIO and agreed to participate in a Steel Workers Organizing Committee (SWOC), which would be controlled by the CIO leadership. Lewis selected Mine Workers vice-president Philip Murray to direct SWOC. Two months later, the CIO unions were expelled from the AFL.

Unlike previous organizing drives in the steel industry, the CIO effort was a big-budget operation. With funds from the Mine Workers and garment unions, SWOC opened 35 regional offices and hired 433 organizers. Headquarters was established on the 36th floor of Pittsburgh's Grant Building, home of corporate offices for several of the major steel firms.

SWOC launched its campaign at a moment when the steel industry was being shaken by a grassroots insurgency from an unlikely source—the company unions, or Employee Representation Plans (ERPs), which most steelmakers had introduced after the National Industrial Recovery Act established a legal foothold for collective bargaining. Employee representatives were generally elected on an annual basis by each department within a mill. Their function was to handle individual grievances, and they were sometimes effective in that respect. But management ceded little power to the "reps" and none to the workers as a body. If the company and the reps could not agree on the resolution of a grievance, the company prevailed. Other than voting in the annual elections, workers had no collective role in the system. Many of them felt that it was not, as one rep put it, "a legitimate form of union."

By 1935, employee reps at U.S. Steel subsidiaries in Pittsburgh and Chicago were agitating for a general

# Steel Workers Win
## Labor Vote Defeats Steel Barons At Polls
### ROOSEVELT RE-ELECTED

You beat the Steel Barons at the polls. YOU Re-elected Roosevelt.
You must now win in the mills, on the job. Organize Your Union.
The power of 500,000 steelworkers, aided by millions of organized labor, proved stronger than the five-billion dollar Iron and Steel Institute. **Four more years of Roosevelt.**
You must finish your job.
The re-election of Roosevelt means four more years of political freedom.
But your political freedom is worth nothing, unless you have industrial democracy and economic freedom to support it.

**ORGANIZE YOUR OWN INDUSTRIAL UNION**

Remarkable progress has already been made. Thousands of steel workers have joined. Dozens of new locals have been set up.
Steel profits increased 139 per cent this year.
The present company union committee is worthless. It is financed and controlled by the bosses.
Your own industrial union is financed and controlled by you.
A wage increase will be granted. Mr. Taylor, the head of U. S. Steel, states that a plan for a wage raise will be announced.
This bears out the Steel Workers Organizing Committee's prediction several weeks ago that steel wages would be raised.
Wages have to be raised. The Steel Workers Organizing Committee is forcing the steel industry to great wage increases and better working conditions.
Your own industrial union and your union's national wage agreement will protect your job, raise your wages, and shorten your hours.
It is legal to organize. President Roosevelt signed laws guaranteeing your right to organize into the union of your own choosing for Collective Bargaining.

**THE WELFARE OF YOUR FAMILY NEEDS A UNION**

The NRA was killed because you were not organized.
Potatoes are dearer, tomatoes are dearer, now is the time to organize. Food costs have jumped 12 per cent since April, 1934.
Stop the favoritism of the petty bosses to their friends and relatives.
Abolish the miserly low wage of 47 cents an hour. How can a family live on $3.76 a day?
Skilled wages are being reduced because unskilled wages are so low.
Prepare America for your children. Demand the decent standard of living you deserve.
You beat the Steel Barons by re-electing Roosevelt. You can beat them again by organizing your own union.
Insure your political freedom. Organize for economic freedom.
Nail this leaflet up in your home. Read it every day before you go to work.

Fraternally yours,

**From the 1890s to the Depression, the mainstream of the labor movement shunned electoral politics. The unprecedented New Deal-CIO coalition signaled a dramatic shift in labor's posture. Above, a SWOC flyer. Below, CIO political headquarters in Shenandoah, PA, 1938.**

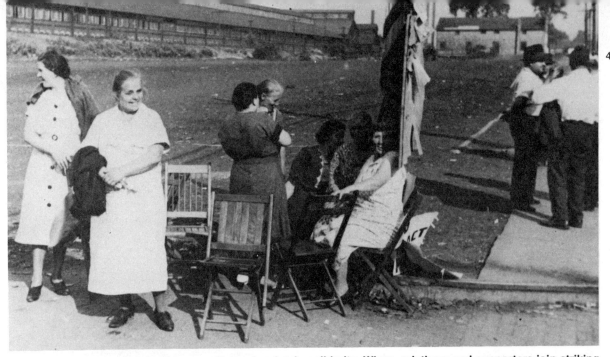

**Pickets serve to publicize labor conflict and maintain solidarity. Wives, relatives, and supporters join striking steelworkers on picket duty.**

wage increase. Management contended that wages were a matter of company-wide policy, outside the jurisdiction of the ERPs. The reps concluded that inter-plant committees were needed.

At Carnegie-Illinois' Duquesne plant, Elmer Maloy and John Kane made inter-plant organizing an issue in the 1935 ERP elections. They won handily, and in January, 80 reps from Duquesne and other Pittsburgh district plants met as a central committee and demanded recognition from the company. At Illinois Steel's South Works in Chicago, George Patterson established the Associated Employees, an independent union which won 22 of the ERP's 36 seats. Reps from other U.S. Steel subsidiaries joined them in an area-wide Calumet Council.

SWOC established contact with Maloy, Kane, Patterson, and other activist reps. Its strategy was to take over the company unions from within, "biting at the heels of management" with demands for a $5 minimum daily wage, a 40-hour work week, and time-and-a-half for overtime. When employee reps were successful in settling grievances, SWOC claimed credit; when they failed, the inadequacies of the ERP system were blamed.

In addition to the ERP machinery ripe for manipulation, SWOC enjoyed an economic and political climate conducive to organizing. The economy was beginning to recover from the depths of the Depression; production was up in the steel industry. A Democratic landslide in 1934 had swept many pro-labor candidates into office. In Pennsylvania, the Governor promised a cheering Labor Day crowd that he would never use troops to break a strike. Congress passed the Wagner Act, increasing the power of the National Labor Relations Board, and the President appointed union sympathizers to serve on it.

Roosevelt was courting organized labor, and the CIO was a willing partner. It boosted membership recruit-

ment with the slogan, "The President wants you to join a union," and it created a political apparatus—Labor's Non-Partisan League—which contributed to Roosevelt's overwhelming reelection in 1936.

Shortly after the election, U.S. Steel offered a contract to its company unions, hoping to undercut the CIO organizing drive. But the offer came too late. CIO activists like Maloy and Patterson, determined to demolish the company union structure, convinced employee reps to reject the contract. In December 1936, 250 reps from 42 U.S. Steel plants met in Pittsburgh and publicly avowed their commitment to SWOC. Murray claimed 125,000 members.

U.S. Steel chairman Myron Taylor saw the handwriting on the wall. His ERPs were collapsing into SWOC, and with a major armaments contract pending with the British government he could ill afford a strike. General Motors, which had financial ties to U.S. Steel, had just signed a contract with the CIO's United Auto Workers after a series of militant "sit-down" strikes, and Taylor sensed that he could not rely on government to intervene on the company's behalf as it had done in the past. On March 2, 1937, after several secret meetings with John L. Lewis, Taylor reversed almost four decades of company policy and approved a preliminary contract with SWOC.

At the signing of the final contract with the Carnegie-Illinois subsidiary a few weeks later, a SWOC representative asked about a picture on the boardroom wall. It occupied the place of an H.C. Frick portrait which had been hastily removed for the occasion. "Didn't think he could stand it," a company representative explained.

The U.S. Steel agreement provided a 10 cents an hour wage increase—sufficient to meet SWOC's five dollars a day demand—as well as a 40-hour work week and

**A novel approach to picketing.**

a union grievance procedure. Its effect on steelworkers was electrifying. In the ten days following the signing, 35,000 new members joined; by the end of April 1937, less than a year after its founding, SWOC had 280,000 members.

But while giant U.S. Steel and its subsidiaries had caved in, the major independents, known as "Little Steel," were holding out. SWOC's organizing penetration in the independents was spotty, especially outside the Pittsburgh district. And Little Steel's leading figure, Republic Steel president Tom Girdler, was a far more combative personality than Myron Taylor.

Girdler's strategy was to provoke a premature strike. In May 1937, he spent $50,000 on munitions, laid off thousands of workers at plants in Canton and Massilon, Ohio, then locked out the remaining Massilon workers. Six days later, SWOC locals in Ohio and Indiana voted to strike. SWOC's national leadership was forced to support them by calling out workers in all Republic, Inland Steel, and Youngstown Sheet and Tube plants that night.

In Chicago, police curtailed picketing, allowing only five or six strikers at Republic's gate and arresting or clubbing others who attempted to join the picket line. Recognizing that the strike would fail without mass picketing, the union called a rally for Sunday, Memorial Day. With American flags leading the parade, several thousand persons, including women and children, began to march toward the plant. Police met them two blocks from the gate and suddenly opened fire. Ten men were fatally shot as they fled. Police beat the fallen and dragged the wounded to paddy wagons.

The violence of the Memorial Day Massacre was exceptional, but police and national guardsmen forcibly disrupted picketing at other Little Steel plants, injuring and arresting hundreds of strikers. The companies sponsored "back to work movements" and "law and order leagues" which raised a public outcry against the strike. Appeals to Roosevelt produced a weak mediating board, which the companies ignored; the frustrated President pronounced "a plague on both your houses." By mid-July, the strike had collapsed. Only at Inland Steel had SWOC secured an agreement, and that did not include union recognition. Elsewhere the strike had failed completely, leaving SWOC at an impasse.

Once again, however, the threat of war intervened on the side of labor, and this time labor was sufficiently well organized to profit from it. As the production of armaments soared prior to American entrance into World War II, the demand for labor increased as well. SWOC and other CIO affiliates launched renewed organizing drives, accompanied by local work stoppages. Concerned about maintaining production, the federal government voiced a hard line against strikers, but it also forced employers to comply with the Wagner Act. By November 1941, SWOC was the recognized bargaining agent for all four major independents.

Industrial unionism owed its triumph to a convergence of factors. Although the CIO's greatest gains occurred during moments of economic recovery, economic collapse was a precipitating force. By exposing the nation to widespread hardship and insecurity, the Depression eroded the pro-business consensus which had ruled American politics since the 1890s. In this fluid climate, employers could no longer depend on the power of the state to suppress the recurrent revolts of rank and file industrial workers. Yet it is unlikely that these factors alone would have produced a significant advance had not Lewis and fellow advocates of industrial unionism recognized the sudden thaw in the organizing climate and thrown caution to the winds in exploiting it.

## MEMORIAL DAY, 1937

"I went down with the front group, right by the flag, and there we met about 650 cops lined up . . . I didn't like it. But I was an organizer in charge of our picket line so I walked along . . . All hell broke loose. I could see the cops there shooting away with their guns. At first I thought they were blanks—I really did. I could smell the gunpowder—I'll never forget it—and then I began to see people fall. Then it dawned on me. They were shooting real bullets. This was for keeps."

George Patterson
SWOC leader

66    THIS MIGHTY DREAM

## Assessing the Bargain

The CIO maintained direct control of SWOC until 1942, when a constitutional convention transformed it into a bona fide union, the United Steelworkers of America (USWA). The union constitution, however, preserved command at the top, granting exceptional powers to the president, including the right to appoint organizers, district directors, and most of the executive committee. It made no provision for membership ratification of contracts and prohibited strikes without the express consent of the president.

Other CIO affiliates, such as the United Auto Workers, adopted more democratic constitutions, but all of the major industrial unions developed centralized, bureaucratic structures in response to the new climate of recognition. Under NLRB supervision, orderly elections and collective bargaining replaced the anarchic battles of the 1930s. Industry-wide contracts solved the problem of organizational maintenance, even assuring financial stability through the mechanism of automatic "dues check-off" from workers' paychecks. In return, union officials made assurances of labor peace.

This bargain undercut the tactical autonomy of the locals. Most contracts abolished or restricted workers' "right to strike." Plant-level grievances which had previously been resolved through immediate rank and file action were consigned to lengthy quasi-judicial procedures. National unions assumed the role of contract enforcers, disciplining locals which defied the ban on "wildcat" walkouts.

"I think we got too much contract," says steelworker Ed Mann. "You hate to be the guy that talks about the good old days but I think the IWW had a darn good idea when they said, 'Well, we'll settle these things as they arise.'"

Lacking a veto over contracts and the right to select their own leaders and staff, steelworkers possessed few means to hold their union accountable. Moreover, the entrenchment of the union hierarchy highlighted a social gap between rank and file members and well-paid national officers, whose excesses were often characterized as "tuxedo unionism." Periodic rank-and-file insurgencies corrected the more flagrant abuses but did not fundamentally alter the top-down character of the USWA.

Strikes and bitter contract disputes punctuated the 1940s and '50s but, by and large, the bargain held. What the militance of the 1930s had won for industrial labor, the more conservative union posture protected: blue collar wages substantially higher than the national median, shorter hours, job security, better working conditions. Through the 1960s, the USWA and other industrial unions prospered. Unprecedented economic growth permitted American companies to grant significant wage and benefit increases without threatening profitability. As industry expanded, union membership grew automatically.

Underneath the boom, however, structural shifts in the U.S. economy were shaking the foundations of labor-management relations, and their impact was suddenly apparent when the economy sputtered in the 1970s. Automation and other technological advances eliminated millions of production jobs, depleting the rolls of the major industrial unions. Competition from low-wage foreign industries and the shift of production from union to non-union shops undermined labor's bargaining position and forced workers to accept wage cuts and other "givebacks" in exchange for job security.

Collective bargaining in the steel industry institutionalized the handling of plant grievances. Above, SWOC sub-regional director Joe Timko (left) listens to local steelworkers president Thomas Peasner (right) describe a grievance which the national union will attempt to mediate, Ambridge, PA, 1941.

The most important shift involved the character of the workforce. By 1960, service occupations employed more workers than manufacturing industries. Although these high-growth occupations spanned an enormous range, from minimum wage cashiers at fast-food restaurants to nurses, teachers, and other white-collar professionals, they did share certain features. By comparison to industrial labor, service workers were disproportionately female, minority, low-paid, and non-union.

Much of the growth in service employment was generated by state and local government, and it was in the public sector that the unions registered their greatest gains after 1960. Despite laws prohibiting them from striking, public employees became the most militant segment of the labor movement; extended walkouts by policemen, teachers, bus drivers, and other public servants secured dramatic wage and benefit increases in dozens of localities. Low wage service workers in the private sector also contributed to union growth. But the gains did not keep pace with the expansion of the workforce; the pro-

In the late 1960s, union drives among low-wage workers harnessed the moral fervor and political resources of the civil rights movement. Above, striking hospital workers rally in Charleston, SC. A sign beside the door reads, "Soul Brothers welcome to Local 1199."

portion of unionized workers in the United States declined from 36 percent in the mid-'50s to less than 25 percent three decades later.

In response to this decline, the old movement battlecry of "Organize the Unorganized" experienced a revival. Public employees, clericals, and workers in the emerging "high-tech" industries were the primary targets, not only for the traditional service sector unions but for hitherto single industry organizations like the Communication Workers of America and the United Auto Workers. The intense competition for new members produced some bruising jurisdictional battles. But it also stimulated the development of sophisticated organizing strategies and collaborative efforts among unions which went beyond the customary gestures of solidarity. A notable example was the joint drive by the Service Employees International Union (SEIU) and the United Food and Commercial Workers (UFCW) to organize the giant Beverly Nursing Homes.

With more than 800 facilities and 60,000 employees, Beverly was the first billion dollar-a-year nursing home chain. The unions devoted a year of research to documenting that the quality of patient care suffered as a result of Beverly's appetite for corporate expansion. Subsequent strategy incorporated patient care issues to build broad public support and to give Beverly workers a sense of "moral authority."

The strategy reflected a deliberate effort to extend the campaign beyond the usually narrow confines of NLRB-supervised elections. In a typical drive, the organizer rushes workers through the process of passing authorization cards and filing for a quick election, with little emphasis on any goal other than representation by the union. With the aid of a new breed of highly paid manage-

The revival of boycott tactics on a national scale boosted union drives in unorganized segments of the workforce. Below, an Atlanta rally uncovers the issues which generated public support for the campaign against the J.P. Stevens textile company.

Clericals, among the fastest growing occupations, were virtually unorganized until groups like 9 to 5 popularized a feminist critique of the white collar workforce. Their success encouraged mainline unions to identify clericals as an organizing priority.

Beverly workers and community supporters picket outside the nursing home chain's annual stockholders meeting. The campaign engineered public confrontations to pressure the company outside the customary channels of labor-management relations.

ment consultants, employers have developed methods to manipulate the NLRB process to their advantage; even if the union wins the vote, contract negotiations are often stalled for months or even years. The traditional organizing style is a poor match for modern union-busting tactics. SEIU and UFCW took a more patient and systematic approach, which relied heavily on worker-to-worker contact to build a solid pro-union core before seeking recognition.

In addition, the unions hit a variety of pressure points which thrust the campaign into public arenas. With support from community organizations and public health associations, they intervened in state regulatory proceedings and the company's annual stockholders meetings. In 1983, the campaign blocked Beverly's expansion plans by holding up $26 million in industrial revenue bonds and stalling state licensing of new facilities. Direct mail and phone solicitation aimed at Beverly stockholders netted a million votes in favor of two union-sponsored resolutions concerning patient care. Even the largest institutional shareholder, Chase Manhattan Bank, was persuaded to side with the union.

The results justified the strategy: by June 1984, the unions had won 35 out of 50 elections representing 6000 Beverly workers, an exceptionally high success ratio. In Texas and Georgia where, as in other Southern states, a fierce anti-union tradition persists, SEIU prevailed in every contest.

Like the nursing home campaign, most major organizing drives today are protracted affairs, and union organizers increasingly stress two strategic elements: building more active rank and file involvement and utilizing intermediate campaigns—most often on workplace issues like health and safety—to win credibility and widen

the base. "It's like the Knights of Labor in the late 1880s," explains Joe Uehlein, an organizer with the AFL-CIO's first coordinated campaign in Tupelo, Mississippi. "Build the enclave of support and move from there."

The parallels to the 1880s are broader. Like the founders of the Knights of Labor, modern labor leaders confront a transformed economic order. With the rise of service sector employment, work has become less centralized. Unlike the huge plants which were the locus of CIO organizing, there are few massive concentrations of labor and, consequently, "action at the point of production" has lost potency. The mobility of capital has reduced labor's leverage; the threat of "runaway shops" looms large at the bargaining table.

In many service industries, there is a greater interaction between public and private sectors. Government regulation offers strategic opportunities, but unions which operate in such vital service sectors as health care and transportation can be crippled in disputes with employers if they fail to command public sympathy. Widespread anti-union sentiment makes this support unreliable and impedes membership recruitment as well. Within the white collar labor force, a blurred distinction between management and labor compounds the problem.

In short, industrial unionism, once a radical innovation, is now as unsuited to the growing sectors of the U.S. economy as craft unionism was to the mass production industries. Some unions have recognized the disastrous potential in this disparity and have attempted to adjust to changing circumstances. But organized labor still possesses political power and recognition, and delivers a measure of prosperity and security to its members. It is hesitant to risk these hard-won gains for a new and uncharted vision of unionism.

# THE BLACK FREEDOM MOVEMENT

## Roots of Resistance

At the dawn of the 20th century, the outlook for black Americans was bleaker than it had been at any time since Emancipation. In the South, where 90 percent of the nation's blacks lived, the "whites-only" primary and other devices had effectively disenfranchised a once-active Negro electorate. Racial segregation was being introduced in schools, streetcars, and public accommodations. The post-Emancipation dream of an independent black yeomanry had been shattered. These setbacks were accompanied by an epidemic of white violence, including the worse outbreak of lynching in the history of the nation.

harsh, and racism was endemic. They did, however, find an environment in which political action was sanctioned and extreme forms of repression, such as lynching, were rare. The density and anonymity of urban life permitted the development of an organized black community and economy which was partially insulated from white control. Urban segregation generated black newspapers, church organizations, colleges, women's clubs, union locals, and a small black professional class to manage these institutions.

From the cities, too, came stirrings of resistance. In 1909, a group of black and white reformers founded the National Association for the Advancement of Colored People to "promote equality of rights and eradicate race prejudice among the citizens of the United States." In the context of that era, it was a radical goal. The NAACP

The burning of William Brown, Omaha, Nebraska, September 28, 1919.

In their struggle to blunt this attack, blacks had no effective allies. The federal government and the Republican Party, their traditional guardians, had made peace with the South and were not willing to intervene. Bold interracial reform movements such as the Farmers Alliance and the Knights of Labor had collapsed in the 1890s, leaving behind conservative trade unionists and embittered Populists who did not wish nor dare to break the color line.

But the edifice of white supremacy was unstable; just as it was completed the seeds of its destruction began to germinate. Seeking jobs and freedom, blacks migrated to the industrial cities of the North. Few found the Promised Land there; jobs were scarce, living conditions were

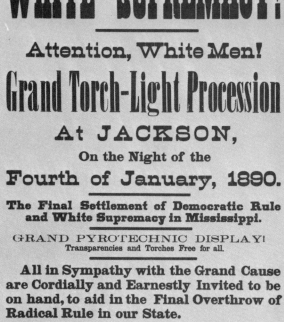

# WHITE SUPREMACY!

## Attention, White Men!

# Grand Torch-Light Procession

## At JACKSON,

On the Night of the

## Fourth of January, 1890.

### The Final Settlement of Democratic Rule and White Supremacy in Mississippi.

GRAND PYROTECHNIC DISPLAY!
Transparencies and Torches Free for all.

**All in Sympathy with the Grand Cause are Cordially and Earnestly Invited to be on hand, to aid in the Final Overthrow of Radical Rule in our State.**

Come on foot or on horse-back; come any way, but be sure to get there.
Brass Bands, Cannon, Flambeau Torches, Transparencies, Sky-rockets, Etc.

A silent protest march against racial violence, New York City, 1917.

The NAACP bravely resisted racial oppression but its high-minded protests had little mass appeal.

used lobbying and litigation to attack the advance of segregation and violence against blacks. But progress was exceedingly slow, and the organization—dominated by professionals—did not develop a mass base within the black community.

In the 1920s, a mass-based organization did emerge among urban blacks. The Universal Negro Improvement Association, led by Marcus Garvey, recruited more than a million members and drew tens of thousands to colorful parades through Harlem and other black neighborhoods. Garvey ridiculed the NAACP's integrationist goals; he called for a return to the African motherland and the creation of an independent black nation. He could not sustain such an ambitious program and the movement collapsed after he was jailed for fraud in 1925. But its forthright appeal to racial pride had struck a responsive chord.

Another critic of the NAACP, from a very different perspective, was A. Philip Randolph. As a socialist, Randolph advocated union organization among black workers and an alliance with the white working classes. He was given an opportunity to test his theories in 1925 when a group of railroad sleeping-car porters—members of a

segregated workforce employed by the Pullman Company—asked for assistance in organizing a union. Within a year, more than half of the Pullman porters had joined the Brotherhood of Sleeping Car Porters, and a decade later, as the industrial union movement transformed labor relations across the country, the Brotherhod won recognition from Pullman and membership in the AFL.

The Depression era proved to be a watershed for black protest. Earlier in the century, blacks had employed direct action sporadically, mounting streetcar and school boycotts in response to the introduction of segregation, and greeting the racist film "Birth of a Nation" with picketing and civil disobedience at theaters. Such protests were isolated and generally unsuccessful. As a rule, the leadership of the black community saw direct action as a defensive, "last resort" tactic, not a viable strategy for change.

In the 1930s, however, blacks took front-line roles in marches, picket lines, anti-eviction actions, and sit-down strikes with such integrated movements as the CIO, the Unemployed Councils, and the Southern Tenant Farmers Union. Late in the decade, "Don't Buy Where

**The Brotherhood of Sleeping Car Porters tapped the growing assertiveness of the black working class.**

Depression era turmoil legitimated direct action tactics. Above, an integrated band of Bonus Marchers. Right, prominent black leader Mary McLeod Bethune (carrying sign) joins a picket line.

You Can't Work" protests erupted in Chicago, Cleveland, New York, and other major cities. Picketers identified ghetto stores which maintained whites-only hiring policies and asked black shoppers to boycott them. These campaigns forced hiring agreements from some merchants and produced a more militant breed of leaders, such as Harlem minister Adam Clayton Powell.

By the end of the decade, the mood of the black masses was assertive and even within the black elite it was respectable to picket and demonstrate in the cause of civil rights. For the first time in half a century, progress seemed possible. Blacks were a growing numerical and political presence in the big cities. Although the Roosevelt Administration had done little to combat racial discrimination, key Administration figures were openly sympathetic to the black cause. The ingredients for a mass movement were in place. The only question was when and how they would be activated.

# The March on Washington Movement

Riding south on a train early in 1941, A. Philip Randolph and his chief aide, Milton Webster, bemoaned job discrimination in the booming defense industries. "I think we ought to do something about it," Randolph said. "I think we ought to get ten thousand Negroes and march down Pennsylvania Avenue asking for jobs in the defense plants and integration of the armed forces. It would shake up Washington."

"And where," Webster asked, "are you going to get ten thousand Negroes?"

It was a reasonable question. There had been no demonstrations of that size in the black community since the Garvey parades. A leading black newspaper, *The Chicago Defender*, insisted that "it is not possible to get Negroes to march in impressive numbers. . . To get 10,000 Negroes assembled in one spot, under one banner . . . would be the miracle of the century."

But Randolph was optimistic. His union members, whose railroad jobs took them around the country, organized "March on Washington" committees and public rallies in dozens of cities. He courted the influential black press, which almost uniformly backed the movement and featured its activities in their pages. As evidence of grass-roots support mounted, Randolph was able to overcome the initial resistance of established black leaders and obtain their endorsements. He asembled a prestigious sponsoring committee, which issued a dramatic call for a July 1st rally at the Lincoln Memorial.

The prospect of a march dismayed the Roosevelt Administration, which was cultivating an image of wartime unity for foreign consumption. "What will they think in Berlin?" one New Dealer asked Randolph. As "March on Washington" buttons went on sale, as scores of ministers urged their flocks to attend, as special trains and buses were chartered, the message from white "friends" in the administration became more urgent: Call off the march! Randolph refused. Finally, in mid-June, he and his allies were summoned to the White House for a meeting.

After some initial sparring, the President asked the group point-blank, "How many people will *really* march?" "One hundred thousand" was Randolph's instant reply. The other black leaders in attendance backed him up. Downplaying the more difficult issue—integration of the armed forces—they hammered on the demand for production jobs. Roosevelt did not commit himself immediately, but a week later he issued Executive Order 8802, which banned discrimination in defense industries

**The March on Washington Movement targeted job discrimination in defense industries during World War II.**

and established a Fair Employment Practices Committee to monitor compliance.

With a victory in hand, Randolph "postponed" the protest indefinitely, although the March on Washington Movement continued its efforts to mobilize the black community. In June 1942, it sponsored a series of giant rallies around the country, drawing 12,000 in Chicago and 18,000 at New York's Madison Square Garden. Randolph issued a public call for civil disobedience protests against segregation. This appeal failed to produce much action; its major effect was to drive away the more conservative leaders. With declining support among the elite, and little action to engage the rank and file, the movement disintegrated.

Nevertheless, Randolph's "magnificent bluff" represented a giant step forward. Although the Fair Employment Practices Committee proved ineffectual, blacks did get more work in the defense industries, particularly as labor shortages became acute in the latter stages of the war. Whatever its actual merits, Executive Order 8802 had been wrested involuntarily from the President of the United States by the threat of direct action. It was the first such victory on a national scale. The March on Washington Movement had demonstrated the strategic value of framing specific, realizable demands and the potential for unified mass protest in the black community.

**Eleanor Roosevelt and A. Philip Randolph promote a 1942 rally at Madison Square Garden.**

10

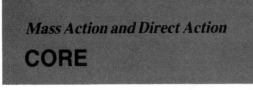

## *Mass Action and Direct Action*
# CORE

Randolph's call for civil disobedience in 1942 received a meager response from the black masses. In the same year, however, a small interracial circle of Chicago university students—members of a Christian pacifist organization named the Fellowship of Reconciliation—launched an unheralded effort to apply the techniques of Mohandas Gandhi to the struggle against racial discrimination.

Gandhi's method, as refined by the Chicago group, consisted of an escalating series of actions directed at a carefully selected target. First came an attempt to convert the adversary through face-to-face negotiation. If reasoning failed, it would be followed by public agitation designed to arouse opinion against the target. Next came direct action tactics, including picketing, boycotts, strikes, and, inspired by the CIO, sit-ins. True civil disobedience—deliberate violation of the law—was the final recourse, avoided in the 1940s but later a hallmark of the civil rights struggle. Practicioners of this method were expected to eschew violence in all cases, no matter what the provocation, and to be guided by the spirit of love for the adversary. The method became known as "nonviolent direct action".

Initial targets were primarily restaurants, amusement parks, theaters, hospitals, and other public accommodations. Although state law prohibited Jim Crow segregation, the group identified two restaurants that refused to serve blacks: Jack Spratt's, near the University of Chicago, and Stoner's, a large downtown establishment. Interracial test groups were received with hostility, seated only after long waits, and served "meat with egg shells scattered on it, or a plate of food salted so heavily that it could not be eaten, or a sandwich composed of lettuce and tomato cores picked out of the garbage can."

After negotiations proved fruitless, group members leafleted outside the restaurant, urging patrons to protest discrimination as they paid their bills. Five months later, with no progress evident, 21 people entered Jack Spratt's together and refused to leave until the blacks in the group were served. The police arrived but declined to intervene, and after two hours the manager capitulated. A larger sit-in at Stoner's produced a similar outcome.

Two Fellowship of Reconciliation staffers, James Farmer and Bayard Rustin, advised and organized similar groups in other Northern cities, and in 1943 these groups formed a national federation, the Congress of Racial Equality (CORE). Reflecting a commitment to local autonomy, the structure of the new organization was highly decentralized. George Houser, a Chicago activist who became CORE's first executive secretary, complained that, "Practically no financial support comes to the national office from the local groups; last year this amounted to $113. . . There is no contact between the national office

**Chicago CORE members picket a segregated apartment building, 1945.**

> "When I look back at that first sit-in, I am amazed at our patience and good faith. No action group today would prolong the attempts at negotiation for more than a month before deciding to demonstrate. No militant Negro today would dream of trying to persuade a manager to serve him on the grounds that Negro patronage would not be bad for business . . . But in those days we were childishly literal-minded . . . We regarded the sit-in as the successful culmination of a long campaign to reach the heart of the restaurant owner with the truth. What we took to be his conversion was as important as the fact that the restaurant had indeed been desegregated."
>
> James Farmer

and the rank and file members. . . It is impossible to support an organization on the basis of this scheme."

By 1947 CORE's leaders had concluded that a national campaign would increase the visibility of the organization and bring the chapters closer together. They proposed a "Journey of Reconciliation" to challenge segregated seating on interstate buses, a practice which continued in the South despite a Supreme Court ruling prohibiting it. The issue offered an opportunity to highlight the shortcomings of the NAACP's legalistic approach and the need for direct action strategies.

Sixteen men, eight white and eight black, boarded buses in Washington, D.C. on April 9, 1947. For two weeks they journeyed through Virginia and North Carolina, refusing to abide by the rule which relegated blacks to the "back of the bus." There were arrests in sev-

76    THIS MIGHTY DREAM

15

Among the interracial group ready to depart on the Journey of Reconciliation in April 1947 are Bayard Rustin (fourth from right) and George Houser (second from right). This first CORE protest in the South was the prototype for the Freedom Rides in 1961.

eral places and one contingent was attacked by a mob near Chapel Hill, North Carolina. Four of the men, including Bayard Rustin, were sentenced to thirty-day stints on a road gang.

Although the Journey of Reconciliation was well publicized, especially in the black press, seating on interstate buses in the South remained segregated. The campaign's immediate organizational impact was modest as well. National CORE continued to be weak and insolvent, if somewhat better known. However, strong new chapters did emerge in some border-state cities, such as Washington, D.C. and St. Louis.

In a six-year campaign, St. Louis CORE desegregated virtually every restaurant associated with downtown dime stores, drugstores, and department stores. As with most local chapters, the activists were an interracial

cadre of young, middle-class men and women, rarely numbering more than a dozen. Tactics were conservative, arrest was shunned, and decorum was stressed. Members were instructed that, "Men are to wear shirts and ties. Correct posture should be remembered."

This pattern of intermittent, small-scale, localized activity was characteristic of CORE through the late '40s and early '50s. By the end of this period, a combination of action, court decisions, and the changing climate of public opinion had made blatant Jim Crow segregation a rarity at public accommodations in Northern and border-state cities. CORE activists identified new targets: employment and housing discrimination in the North, public accommodations in the South. But to attack these issues, where both the law and public opinion were less favorable, CORE needed a mass constituency in the black com-

17

16

**Members of the Interracial Workshop, a CORE affiliate in Washington, D.C., plot strategy to challenge segregation at cafeterias in church-owned and public buildings.**

munity. After more than a decade of activity, it still did
not have one.

Organizational weakness certainly had circumscribed CORE's hopes of sparking a mass movement; with little money, staff, or national coordination,
it was hard to deliver the message to a mass audience. But
the message itself was problematic. CORE's earnest,
middle-class tone, its philosophical pacifism, its strenu-
ous interracialism were not especially suited to a working-class black constituency. Instead, as founder Bernice
Fisher noted, the organization often attracted individuals
"more interested in being nonviolent than in hitting the
race question." Finally, sit-ins and other direct action tactics seemed excessively dangerous during this period
when the political temper of the nation was more conservative than it had been since the 1920s. For most blacks,
the spectre of white repression was very real, and they
were not yet ready to defy it.

# The Montgomery Bus Boycott

While grassroots agitation for civil rights measures diminished, the struggle against segregation advanced rapidly on another front. Responding to lawsuits mounted by
the NAACP, state and federal courts delivered a series of
blows to Jim Crow, culminating in the 1954 Supreme
Court decision in *Brown v. Board of Education* declaring
"separate but equal" schools unconstitutional.

*Brown* had little immediate impact on school segregation, but it put an indelible stamp of legitimacy on the
civil rights cause. In its wake Southern blacks began to
mobilize. The first major battle unfolded in "The Cradle
of the Confederacy"—Montgomery, Alabama—where
the black community organized an extraordinary 381-day
boycott of the city bus lines.

Modernization and urbanization in the South, ac-
celerating after World War II, replicated many of the conditions which had previously fostered mass protest in the
North. Although Montgomery's 50,000 black citizens
continued to face blatant discrimination, some found new
prosperity and independence. From the growing middle
class emerged a core of activists dedicated to fighting Jim
Crow. Most prominent among them was E.D. Nixon, regional officer of the Brotherhood of Sleeping Car Porters,
veteran of the March on Washington Movement, and
former state president of the NAACP.

The facade of segregation was no longer uniform in
Montgomery. Maxwell Air Force Base, a major local employer, was integrated, and the new municipal coliseum
had been designed without the usual provisions for separate seating, entrances, and restrooms. City buses, on the
other hand, symbolized the worst indignities of Jim
Crow. Blacks were not only barred from the front section;
they were routinely ordered to give up seats in the unre-
served middle section to white passengers. Many drivers
were rude and openly racist.

E.D. Nixon had long harbored a plan to challenge
segregated seating on the buses, a notion he shared with
Jo Ann Robinson and fellow members of the Women's
Political Council, the black counterpart to the all-white
Montgomery League of Women Voters. With a black
ridership of at least 70 percent, the privately-owned bus
company was vulnerable to a racial boycott.

On Thursday, December 1, 1955, a black seamstress
named Rosa Parks was riding the bus home from work
when the driver ordered her to relinquish her seat to a
white man. She refused and was arrested. There had been
similar incidents before—three in the previous year—but
when Rosa Parks was taken to jail, Nixon knew he had
the perfect test case. Parks had been secretary of the
NAACP, she possessed an unimpeachable character,
and, in Nixon's judgment, "she wasn't afraid and she
didn't get excited about anything." Her calm demeanor

## 18

**Rosa Parks, whose refusal to relinquish her seat sparked the Montgomery bus boycott, is fingerprinted at police headquarters.**

forced city officials to charge her with violating the segregation law rather than the customary charge of disorderly conduct, setting the stage for a head-on legal challenge.

Nixon was more immediately concerned with mass action. On the following day he called black ministers to a meeting at a downtown church pastored by a recent arrival from Atlanta, 26-year-old Martin Luther King, Jr. Nixon handpicked the young minister to lead the struggle, reasoning that as a newcomer King was not yet beholden to city officials nor entangled in local leadership rivalries.

By evening the Women's Council had distributed 40,000 flyers saying: "Don't ride the bus to work, to town, to school or anywhere on Monday. If you work, take a cab, share a ride or walk." Nixon tipped off Joe Azbell, a white reporter he had been cultivating, and the Sunday *Montgomery Advertiser* carried a front-page article on the impending boycott. Ministers reinforced the message from their pulpits. Black cab drivers were hastily enlisted to provide rides at the cost of busfare.

On Monday the boycott was virtually one hundred percent effective. Nearly 7000 people packed a church for a meeting that night, spilling into the adjacent streets where the proceedings were broadcast by loudspeaker. The assembly approved a proposal to maintain the boycott, establishing the Montgomery Improvement Association (MIA) to conduct it and electing King as MIA president.

"I got up the next morning at five o'clock and started calling people. I called Ralph D. Abernathy, and he said, 'Yeah, Brother Nixon, you know I'll go along with you.' And then I called Rev. H.H. Hubbard, and he said, 'Yeah, Brother Nixon, I'll go along with you'. . . Then the third person I called was Martin Luther King. He said, 'Brother Nixon, let me think about it awhile and call me back. And I called him back. He said, 'Yeah, Brother Nixon, I decided, I'm going to go along with you.' And I said, 'That's fine, because I called 18 other people and I told them they're going to meet at your church this evening."

E.D. Nixon

# The Montgomery Advertiser

ALABAMA JOURNAL Combined Dec. 1, 1950

Montgomery, Ala., Sunday Morning, December 4, 1955     9 Sections—86 Pages     15 Cents—Pay No M

27th Year No. 46

The Weather

Montgomery. Partly cl with scattered showers an der showers Predicted h today 79, low 80. High var 80, low 53 (Details. Weather Page 8D.)

## School Issue In Spotlight On Long Ballot

### Voters To Decide On 29 Amendments At Polls Tuesday

Alabama voters will go to the polls Tuesday to decide the fate of 29 proposed amendments to the state constitution, including two which if ratified will finance a record-shattering school program.

The long ballot to greet the voters at the polling places include six amendments of statewide application and 23 which are purely local, affecting either one or two counties or cities.

Practically all of the interest leading up to the referendum has centered around Amendments No. 1 and No. 2. Amendment No. 1 is the proposed Goodwyn liquor tax, and No. 2 is the $110,000,000 bond issue to be used in a school construction program.

**ADJUSTED INCOME**

The Goodwyn tax as proposed would be a levy on the "adjusted gross incomes" of individuals and corporations, and would produce an estimated $20,000,000 annually for education.

Rep. O. J. (Joe) Goodwyn of Montgomery county, author of the bill, has defined "adjusted income" as all such income excluding normal business expenses, or expense which is necessary in providing the income.

He has further described his plan as a "net profits tax" and not a gross profits tax.

The proposed bond issue is to be financed by the Goodwyn plan, and should the tax proposal be rejected it would be necessary for the Legislature to find sufficient financing revenue elsewhere before the bonds could be issued.

Here is a brief explanation of the remaining amendments on the ballot:

Amendment No. 3: This proposal would permit any county or school district in the state to levy an additional property tax, with the proceeds earmarked for education. Under the present law, each school district or county will have to increase its property tax if it wishes first have to be approved by the entire state.

Amendment No. 4: Similar to No. 3.

(See SCHOOL, Page 6A)

## Legal Forum Set Tuesday

A discussion of "The Law of Neighbors" will be featured on the Montgomery Bar Assn.-Advertiser-Journal Legal Forum at 7.30 p.m. Tuesday.

Panel members who are attorneys and their discussion will include:

Robert Varner: nuisances, including smells, noises and animals, covering obnoxious dogs and cats.

Evans Hinson: trees, fences, and parting walls, and hedges including spite fences.

Sol Brinsfield: easement including land driveways, drainage and the flow of water.

Frank Hawthorne: zoning and plat restrictions and restrictive covenants.

Moderator will be Sam Rice Baker. The program will be held in the Montgomery County Courthouse and is free to the general public.

## 'PICKENS COUNTY MOSES?'

Rev. and Mrs. Rayburn Ray wait confidently as they point out Tuesday, Dec. 6, on the calendar. It's the date the Lowndes county referendum to make the county dry comes before the people. Ray, of Pickens County, has been leading the campaign to return Lowndes to a dry state.—Photo by Lesher

### MINISTER LEADING WAY

# Lowndes County Voters Weigh Wet-Dry Question

By GERRY LEE
Advertiser Assistant Managing Editor

FORT DEPOSIT, Ala., Dec. 3 — A slender 30-year-old Baptist minister from Gordo, Ala., hopes to be the Pickens County Moses that leads Lowndes County out of the wilderness of state-controlled alcoholic beverage sales come Tuesday's election.

The Rev. Rayburn Ray, who fills the pulpit at Fort Deposit's Bethel Baptist Church each Sunday, decided this Black Belt county needed "drying up" last September after two county raids spearheaded by J. M. Sweeney of the Alabama Temperance Alliance.

**SLIDE DOOR**

Success for Ray at the polls Tuesday would slam the door on the county's only liquor store at Fort Deposit and dry up a few scattered beer joints.

It was Ray who led the crusade through the red clay hills of Lowndes in getting enough names on a petition to force a showdown on the wet-dry question.

Lowndes, which has been wet since a state election on Nov. 10, 1937, puts the issue before the county's voters for the first time since that date. It was in 1937 that the wets managed a victory by only 78 votes.

They proudly point out the petition needed only 234 names to put the issue to test. Ray's crew of busy-beating Baptist and Methodist laymen stirred up a list of 591 signatures.

The Pickens parson submitted the petition to Lowndes Probate Judge Harrell Hammonds at the county seat in Haynesville on Nov. 3.

**ABC BOARD CHIEF**

Hammonds, ironically, is the Folsom-appointed chairman of Alabama's Alcoholic Beverage Control Board.

In the light of Judge Hammonds' position with the state ABC board has he taken an active role against Ray's dry crusade?

Ray says not. "To my knowledge Judge Hammonds took no active part either way."

The young minister says his own position in Tuesday's election was influenced only by "the moral issue."

He says, there have been as many incidents from a phase standpoint...

"There was a rumor I had to (See LOWNDES, Page 6A)

## Dec. 3 Heat Snaps Record

Warm winds from the Gulf of Mexico precipitated the warmest Dec. 3 in Montgomery's history, according to the U.S. Weather Bureau at Dannelly Field.

The mercury rose to an unseasonal 80 degrees shortly after 2 p.m. yesterday breaking the record of 78 degrees set Dec. 3. The all-time high for this time of the year in Montgomery is 83 degrees set on Dec. 7, 1951.

A rainfall of .15 inch added discomfort to the heat as the humidity ranged as high as 93 per cent for the day was 53 degrees. The low temperature reading for the day was 53 degrees.

Unusual heat prevailed throughout the state with Dothan reporting a high of 81 degrees and evergreen a high of 80. There was rainfall sprinkled over Alabama.

Weathermen forecast a partly cloudy and warm day today with scattered showers and thundershowers. They added it will turn cool late tonight. The predicted high is 78 degrees while the low is forecast as 60.

## Army Speeds Rotation Of Troops In Far East

SEOUL, Sunday, Dec. 4 (AP)—The U.S. Army said today it is speeding up its usual rotation of soldiers scheduled for the United States to get as many as possible home for Christmas.

Since mid-November, the Army reported, 3,300 U.S. soldiers have left Korea for home. Another 1,890, who normally would leave in January, will depart by mid-December.

## FAVORITE SON

# Harriman Up For Nomination But Status Still 'Inactive'

OKLAHOMA CITY, Dec. 3 (AP)—Gov. Averell Harriman of New York today had his name still up in nomination for president at the 1956 Democratic national convention but continued to insist he is an active candidate.

...gather and decide what are the...

Harriman said his name will not be entered in any preferential primary. Stevenson, who spoke to the Young Democrats yesterday...

# Angry Mob Of Tech Student Protests Griffin Bowl Stan

## Demonstrators Smash Line Of Police At State Capitol

By JIM THOMASSON

ATLANTA, Dec. 3 (AP)—Gov. Marvin Griffin's official residence and the Georgia State Capitol were stormed early today by a howling mob of Georgia Tech students angered by Griffin's move to keep Tech out of the Sugar Bowl.

The demonstrators, who several times burned Griffin in effigy, broke through a cordon of Georgia Bureau of Investigation agents and smashed their way into the Capitol.

But police lines reinforced with 26 cars of state troopers held back the crowd of more than 2,000 at the governor's mansion.

**REQUEST TO REGENTS**

The demonstration was touched off by Griffin's message to the university system Board of Regents to bar state colleges from playing opponents having Negro players or in games where spectators are not racially segregated.

Pittsburgh has a Negro, Bobby Grier, a reserve back, on its football squad. And segregation will not be practiced in the sale of Pitt's bloc of tickets to the Jan. 2 game in the Sugar Bowl in New Orleans.

A few hours after the student demonstration broke up, a source close to the governor, who declined to be quoted by name, said, "Georgia Tech will be allowed to play in the Sugar Bowl."

**DIDN'T MENTION BOWL**

This Griffin administration source pointed out that the governor's message to Regent Chairman Robert O. Arnold of Covington did not specifically mention the Sugar Bowl.

But in view of the sweeping segregation policy laid down by the governor and his call of "an immediate called meeting" of the regents to consider it, the request obviously was prompted by the forthcoming bowl game.

Arnold said today he has asked the regents to meet at 11:30 a.m. Monday to study the governor's request.

But in addition to the administration spokesman's statement, there were other indications that Tech's Sugar Bowl contract will not be disturbed.

**CLOSE FRIENDS**

Regent Quimby Melton, editor of the Griffin Ga., News and a close friend of the governor, first declined to comment on the matter, but later apparently laid down the administration's policy line. He suggested that Tech be allowed to carry out its Sugar Bowl contract, but that the regents adopt Griffin's suggestion for all future athletic events of state colleges.

Tech President Blake Van Leer told John Earp, Chicago NBC sports editor in telephone interview, "I'm 60 years old and I have never broken a contract and I'm not going to break one now."

Van Leer, also is chairman of the Tech Athletic Corporation, a separate agency set up by the Legislature to handle athletic affairs.

The race issue in connection with the Sugar Bowl was raised unofficially earlier in the week when Hugh G. Grant of Augusta, former diplomat and fervent prosegregationist, wired Tech coach Bobby Dodd a protest.

Dodd ignored it and Arnold at that time said it would be "no innovation" for Tech to play against a Negro.

## YOUNG DEMOS NIX METCALF

OKLAHOMA CITY, Dec. 3 (AP)—David Bunn of Denver was elected president of the Young Democrats of America over Neil Metcalf, Geneva, Ala., at the organization's national convention here.

Bunn received 500 votes to 380 for Metcalf, William Poindexter of Kansas City, the third candidate, was never in the running.

The new president succeeds Neal Smith of Des Moines, Iowa.

## Negro Groups Ready Boycott Of City Lines

By JOE AZBELL
Advertiser City Editor

A "top secret" meeting of Montgomery Negroes who plan a boycott of city buses Monday is scheduled at 7 p.m. Monday at the Holt Street Baptist Church for "further instructions" in a "massive nonviolent" campaign against segregation on city busses, the Advertiser learned last night.

The campaign, modelled along the lines of the White Citizens Council program, was initiated by unidentified Negro leaders after a Negro woman, Rosa Parks, was arrested by city police Thursday on a charge of violating segregation laws by sitting in the white section of a city bus.

Yesterday Negro sections were flooded with thousands of copies of mimeographed or typed letters asking Negroes to refrain from riding city busses Monday.

**SECOND TIME**

The letter stated:

"Another Negro woman has been arrested and thrown into jail because she refused to get up out of her seat on the bus and give it to a white person. It is the second time since the Claudette Colbert case that a Negro has been arrested for the same thing. This must be stopped. Negroes are citizens and have rights.

"Until we do something to stop these arrests, they will continue. The next time it may be you, or you or you. This woman's case will come up Monday. We are, therefore, asking every Negro to stay off the busses on Monday in protest of the arrest and trial. Don't ride the busses to work, to town, to school or anywhere on Monday. You can afford to stay out of school for one day if you have no other way to go except by bus. If you work, take a cab or walk, but please children and grownups, don't get on a bus at

(See NEGRO, Page 6A)

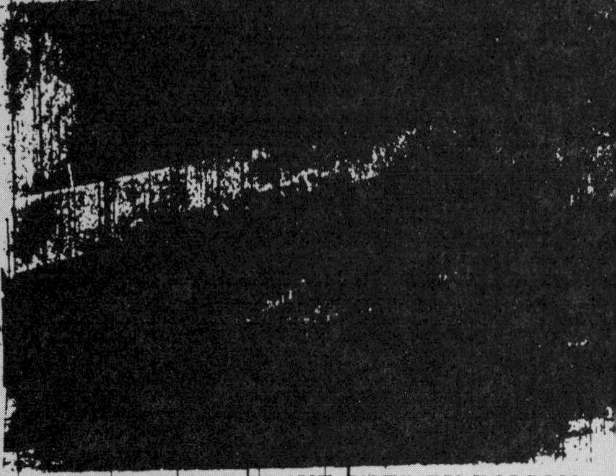

## TENNESSEE PLANE USED BY FOLSOM

This Tennessee National Guard C-47 was the plane used by Gov. James E. Folsom in his trip to Mobile to Oklahoma City Friday. The Tennessee plane was loaned to Folsom after the Alabama Guard's C-47, "The Gully Jumper" was put in the shop for an overhaul. This photo was taken at Dannelly Field by Bob Underwood, announcer-photographer for WCOV-TV.

# Tennessee Air Guard Confirms Repo Folsom Made Trip In Borrowed Plan

By BOB INGRAM

The Tennessee Air Guard in Memphis confirmed yesterday that one of its planes had been loaned to Gov. James E. Folsom for use in flying him to the Young Democrats national convention in Oklahoma City.

The plane, a C-47, was loaned to Alabama on the request of Adj. Gen. William D. Partlow Jr., after Alabama's C-47, "The Gully Jumper," normally used by Folsom, was grounded for repairs.

The Tennessee C-47 picked up Folsom at Brookley Field in Mobile Thursday, after first having landed at Dannelly Field Wednesday afternoon.

While on the runway at Dannelly a photograph was made of the plane, and as a result of this picture the cameraman reportedly was threatened with legal action by an Air Guard official.

Bob Underwood, an announcer and photographer for WCOV-TV here, took the picture of the plane shortly after he had landed his own light plane nearby.

"I had been out flying and just was landing at Dannelly. I heard over my radio a conversation between the C-47 and the ground," Underwood said. "The C-47 pilot radioed to the field asking where he was to pick up the two governors."

Dannelly Field radioed back asking what governors the pilot was talking about, Underwood continued. "The pilot then replied, 'Folsom and Harriman.' The ground radio then replied it knew nothing about it, and suggested the plane land near the Air Guard hanger.

"After hearing this conversation I hopped out of my plane, grabbed my camera and ran over to get a picture of the two governors." Underwood continued. "When they

(See TENNESSEE, Page 6A)

didn't show up. I went and took a picture of the plane.

Underwood said later he got a phone call from Ed Dom, former manager of the shopping center who he was employed as an information writer for the state, by the Air Guard official.

"Dombrowski wanted to know what I took a picture of when I told him, he plane was on a confidential instrument calibration and no pictures should be taken without permission," Underwood continued. "I asked if it was necessary to fly to Mobile for such a way, when it could have been as easily on a flight to or Chattanooga. He said I know about that."

(See TENNESSEE, Page 6A)

## State Counts 8 Lives Lost On Highways

By THE ASSOCIATED PRESS

At least eight persons died in weekend traffic accidents in Alabama.

A four-year-old Robertsdale girl was killed and eight other persons hurt Trussville, Ala., in a head-on collision of two cars near Foley, Ala.

Brenda Sue Boyington, daughter of Mr. and Mrs. Doyle Boyington, died shortly after she was taken to a Foley hospital. Her parents were among the injured.

**DIED SATURDAY**

Dickey Layfield, 17, Springville, Rt. 2, died Saturday when a car in which he was a passenger was wrecked near Trussville, Ala., Friday night. William Herschel Vaughn, 28, St. Clair County, died earlier after being injured in the same accident.

Another traffic accident which caused two deaths occurred before the weekend period began at 6 p.m. Friday.

Mrs. Hazel Lewis Cox, 42, Clanton, and McKinley Barber, 53, Wetumpka, were killed in the headon collision of two automobiles 5.2 miles north of Wetumpka on Highway 111 Friday afternoon.

(See TRAFFIC, Page 6A)

## Clifton E. Oliver Dies At Age Of 78

DADEVILLE, Ala., Dec. 3 (Special)—Clifton E. Oliver, mayor of Dadeville from 1918 to 1940, died in Alexander City today after an illness of several days. He was 78.

Born and educated in Tallapoosa County, Oliver was a director of Alabama Mills and the bank of Dadeville at the time of his death. He was prominent in religious and civic affairs through throughout his active years.

Funeral services will be held from the Dadeville Methodist Church at 2 p.m. Sunday with the Rev. Carl E. Folsom officiating. Burial will be in Dadeville Cemetery.

## API Gets $650,000 For 2 New Dorms

WASHINGTON, Dec. 3 (AP)—A loan of $650,000 to the Alabama Polytechnic Institute, Auburn, Ala., to build two dormitories, was announced today by the Community Facilities Administration.

One dormitory will house 100 women students and the other 150 male students.

Auburn, on the ...

## $16,000 Pl Ready For By Govern

A 1955 Cessna airplane has been purchased from the falconia dealer for $16,000 by Gov. James E. Folsom for Montgomery.

It also was reported a ... of was traded in and $16,0... and given for the plane. The old model is said to be repurchased by the sta... price of $10,000.

According to reliable ... new plane cannot change... but separately the pl... ped here permanently. The was not satisfactory and was moved for new equipment.

The highway department proposed to have use of the new and reliable sources at a ... and reliable purchase ... been approved by Hw... director Herman Nelsng... plane would be used ... work.

## EYES ON GETTYSBURG

# 2 Republican Leaders Di On Outlook For Second T

Gettysburg, Pa., Dec. 3 (AP)—The Republican over whether President Eisenhower will run ... best term differed here today as ... leaders of Congress...

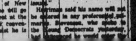

## 19

**The organization of a carpool system by black churches was a critical factor in the success of the boycott.**

The MIA's initial demands were modest: courteous treatment of passengers, hiring of black drivers for predominantly black routes, and a modified form of seat segregation. But the bus company and city leaders refused to compromise. "If we grant Negroes these demands, they would go about boasting of a victory that they have won over the white people, and this we will not stand for," stated the company's lawyer. Few whites believed that the boycott would last.

The City's strategy was to hasten the inevitable through legal harassment. One threat was the enforcement of an ordinance requiring taxis to charge minimum fares. To circumvent it, the MIA established an elaborate carpool system employing 150 volunteer drivers and dozens of dispatch and collection sites. City police then ticketed drivers for minor infractions and threatened to apply vagrancy ordinances to people waiting for rides. Building inspectors displaced the MIA office four times until it was finally established in a hall owned by a black bricklayers' local. More than 100 black leaders were indicted for violating an Alabama anti-boycott statute.

None of these tactics was successful. The boycott continued, the bus company and downtown merchants sustained heavy losses, and the MIA raised the stakes by demanding complete desegregation of the buses. Whites reacted by hardening their opposition to desegregation; membership in the local Citizens Council, described by a *Montgomery Advertiser* editor as "manicured Ku Klux Klansmen," soared from 800 to 13,000 during the course of the boycott.

On January 30, a bomb exploded under King's house. Unhurt, the young pastor may have averted a riot by imploring an angry crowd of followers to eschew retaliation and "love your enemies."

"The mayor said as soon as the first rainy day came, all the blacks would be back on the buses and glad to get back on. The first day it rained it was a sight to see—people just walking in the rain, water dripping off of them, soaked but they just kept walking."

Johnny Carr

**Martin Luther King, Jr. (left) and Bayard Rustin (right). Rustin brought to Montgomery a working knowledge of Gandhian principles which influenced the development of King's nonviolent philosophy.**

King's response was both Christian and pragmatic; a rampaging black mob would have provoked a brutal reaction. Yet, according to CORE veteran Bayard Rustin, who came from New York City to advise him, "Dr. King was not a confirmed believer in nonviolence, totally, at the time the boycott began. On my second visit there the house was still being protected by armed guards." Through reading, reflection, and discussion with Rustin, King forged the distinctive amalgam of Christianity and Gandhian nonviolence which would guide him for the remainder of his life.

Rustin's involvement reflected the intense national and international interest aroused by the Montgomery campaign. Money poured into the MIA from Northern civil rights groups, the UAW and other unions, and countless individuals. The organizers used much of it to purchase and fuel a fleet of station wagons for the carpool.

Against all odds the boycott held firm through the winter, spring, and summer of 1956, parrying the opposition at every turn; when Southern insurers refused to underwrite the carpools, the MIA obtained a policy from Lloyds of London. Finally, in late October, the City sought an injunction to halt the carpool, a strategy which might have broken the boycott. But before the injunction was granted, word arrived that the U.S. Supreme Court had struck down Alabama's bus segregation laws. On December 21, 1956, King and other boycott leaders boarded the first integrated bus in Montgomery without incident.

The Montgomery bus boycott was not, as many believe, the first of its kind; blacks in Baton Rouge, Louisiana, had conducted a similar campaign in 1953 without attracting much attention. And it was the Supreme Court, not the boycotters, which forced desegregation. Yet the impact of Montgomery was enormous. It in-

## INTEGRATED BUS SUGGESTIONS

The *whole* bus is now for the use of *all* people. Take a vacant seat.

Do not deliberately sit by a white person, unless there is no other seat.

If cursed, do not curse back. If pushed, do not push back. If struck, do not strike back, but evidence love and goodwill at all times.

If you feel you cannot take it, walk for another week or two.

Remember this is not a victory for Negroes alone, but for all Montgomery, and the South. Do not boast! Do not brag!

Be quiet but friendly; proud, but not arrogant; joyous, but not boiserous.

from a leaflet distributed by MIA

The boycott commanded national and international attention. Below, white newsmen crowd around MIA leaders at a mass prayer meeting.

21

**Integrating the buses, December 21, 1956.**

spired a new mood among Southern blacks, a willingness to challenge Jim Crow and suffer the consequences. It crystallized the growing Northern sentiment against racial segregation. And it catapulted Martin Luther King, Jr. and his associates into prominence.

In 1957 King and other black Southern ministers founded the Southern Christian Leadership Conference (SCLC) to extend the techniques and nonviolent philosophy of the Montgomery campaign to new communities. But the SCLC moved cautiously. It was Southern whites who seized the offensive in the late 1950s, launching a grassroots campaign of massive resistance to court-ordered desegregation.

In the face of inflammatory rhetoric, mob violence, and the obdurate refusal of local officials to implement court orders, national political leaders vacillated. Democrats faced a widening chasm between their party's two largest electoral bases: the urban North, with its growing blocs of black voters, and the once-solid South, increasingly swayed by hard-line racist appeals. Republicans were torn between the GOP's traditional support for civil rights and the tempting prospect of reaping gains in Dixie at the Democrats' expense. As a new decade opened in 1960, it appeared doubtful that the nation possessed the political will to force a recalcitrant South to comply with the law.

**The emergence of mass protest in the South placed the Democratic Party in an untenable position, as it tried to accommodate both white segregationists and civil rights advocates.**

## 23

## Southern Battlefields
# Sit-ins and Freedom Rides

On February 1, 1960, four freshmen at all-black North Carolina A&T College in Greensboro launched an impulsive protest against racial discrimination at the lunch counter of a downtown Woolworth's store. Influenced by Gandhi's teachings, though unaware of CORE's earlier campaigns, they took seats at the counter and ordered coffee and pie. Refused service, they stayed until closing time and returned the next day with 26 others. Within a week, hundreds of students were taking shifts at sit-in protests in Woolworth's and other segregated establishments.

News of the Greensboro sit-ins ignited campuses across the South. The historically conservative black colleges, dependent on state legislatures and white donors for financial survival, were an unlikely fount of social upheaval. But they harbored a growing cadre of students, like John Lewis in Nashville, who had been galvanized by the Montgomery bus boycott and awaited an opportunity to act.

Lewis belonged to a study group on nonviolent direct action, which had mounted a test sit-in at a local de-

partment store in late 1959. "So the call from North Carolina really didn't find a vacuum," Lewis says. The response was equally rapid in Atlanta and other collegiate centers. Among upwardly mobile black youth, the sit-in movement tapped a hidden reservoir of frustration with the glacial pace of racial progress.

With few exceptions, the protestors adhered strictly to the principles of nonviolence. Their demeanor impressed white sympathizers and editorialists, but store owners and bystanders often reacted brutally. One out of ten students participating in the sit-in movement during the first year was clubbed, beaten, gassed, or burned. One of every six was arrested.

Arrest was no longer an effective deterrent, however. Bernard Lafayette, a leader of the Nashville sit-in movement, remembers students lining up to get arrested, "because they wanted to be part of the movement and that's what it meant. Being part of the movement was putting your body in the movement. Matter of fact, it was no fun being out of jail when all your friends were in jail. That's where the action was."

By mid-April, 50,000 protestors had mobilized in 78 communities; 2000 had been arrested. Established civil rights organizations—the NAACP, SCLC, and CORE—were anxious to direct and absorb the burgeoning movement. SCLC Executive Director Ella Baker organized an

**A student sit-in at a Woolworth lunch counter in Jackson, Mississippi.**

24

Easter weekend conference in Raleigh, North Carolina, attended by 120 Southern sit-in leaders and nearly 100 observers, many of them white, from Northern student groups.

Baker, an experienced behind-the-scenes organizer, brought a mixed agenda to the Raleigh conference. She agreed with other veteran activists that the sit-in movement was narrow and directionless, and she urged the students to seek "more than a hamburger," to think politically and strategically. But Baker saw the impetuous students as an antidote to the caution of established leaders, including her own colleagues at SCLC, who had failed to capitalize on the Montgomery breakthrough and the restive mood of the black South. With her encouragement, the Raleigh conferees established an independent organization, the Student Nonviolent Coordinating Committee (SNCC—pronounced "Snick").

As Baker had hoped, the student movement rapidly acquired a strategic perspective. In Atlanta, students timed a major sit-in at Rich's department store to coincide with the climax of the 1960 presidential election campaign and convinced a reluctant Martin Luther King, Jr. to get arrested with them. King was sentenced to four months at a maximum security prison. A sympathy call to King's wife from candidate John Kennedy and a plea for clemency from Robert Kennedy made the arrest a na-

**Established civil rights groups organized picket lines at Northern Woolworth stores to support the student movement.**

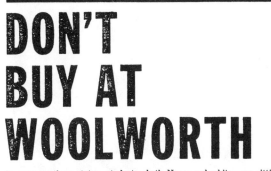

# DON'T BUY AT WOOLWORTH

In many southern states—students—both Negro and white—are sitting in at lunch counters, quietly but persistently demanding that Woolworth serve everyone—regardless of color.

**THESE STUDENTS FACE:**

Mass arrests. . . . Exhorbitant fines. . . . Threats of expulsion from school. In some cases, they sit while segregationist hoodlums brandish knives, hammers and baseball bats. Yet,

**WOOLWORTH CAN SERVE**

Discriminatory seating in most cases is *NOT* required by law. Even where such laws exist, they are obviously unconstitutional. In a matter of minutes, Woolworth management in New York City can direct its southern stores to serve everyone.

**YOU CAN MAKE WOOLWORTH SERVE**

This and every other Woolworth store is directly controlled by the national chain. Every dime and dollar spent here is an open endorsement of the chain's policy of racial segregation and discrimination. *DON'T BACK SOUTHERN SEGREGATION WITH YOUR MONEY.*

**DON'T BUY AT WOOLWORTH**

*JOIN CORE'S PICKET LINES.* Ask all other men of goodwill not to shop jimcrow.

 **CORE** Congress of Racial Equality
38 Park Row, New York 38, New York
COrtlandt 7-0408

"Let me tell you where I was looking at. In 1959, I believe it was, in Oklahoma or somewhere, some kids down there in the NAACP had been involved in a kind of sit-in, but it never spread. And my position was that the situation in Greensboro would be another isolated incident in black history if others didn't join in . . . In really analyzing it, the only people in the black community at that time who were free to take on the Establishment were college kids."

Lonnie King
Atlanta sit-in leader

**Agenda for the Raleigh conference of sit-in leaders which spawned SNCC, April, 1960.**

 26

```
    8:45 - 10:00 A.M.        Committee Hour
   10:00 - 12:30             Plenary Session - Findings and Recom-
                                  mendations.
   12:30 -  1:00 P.M.        P R E S S   C O N F E R E N C E
            1:00 P.M.              L U N C H E O N


         A R E A S   O F   D I S C U S S I O N

        The student Sit-In movement holds great potential for social
change.  The Easter weekend meeting is designed to evaluate what has
happened, why it happened, and what the next steps are, in the drive
for human dignity.  Many questions have been raised, and the following
are suggestive of the points to be explored by the Student Leadership
Conference:

        1.  Advantages and Disadvantages: of Mass Demonstrations
                                    of Small Sit-Ins.
        2.  "Jail vs Bail" ..... Going to Jail with a Purpose
        3.  Where Picketing and Economic Pressure are Useful
        4.  Dangers, Limitations, and Potentials of the Legal
            Approach.
        5.  Philosophy and Techniques of Nonviolence.


 C O M M I T T E E S :

        The following committees seem desirable, and we hope that all
students will come prepared to serve where needed:

            1.  Steering Committee
            2.  Reporting Committee (To cover workshop discussions)
            3.  Committee on Findings and Recommendations.
            4.  Press Committee
            5.  Devotions Committee


 A R R I V A L  -  I M P O R T A N T !

        Please try to arrive Friday, in time for the 4:00 P.M. Press
Conference; but by all means, in time for the opening meeting.
```

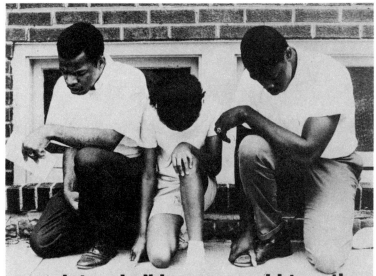

come let us build a new world together
STUDENT NONVIOLENT COORDINATING COMMITTEE 8½ RAYMOND STREET, N.W. ATLANTA 14, GEORGIA

27

tional incident, and the resulting increase in black support contributed to Kennedy's narrow election victory a few weeks later.

By the end of 1960, the wave of sit-ins had crested. Dozens of establishments in Greensboro, Nashville, Atlanta, and other upper South cities had been compelled to integrate. But elsewhere in the region, in Mississippi, Alabama, south Georgia, and the rural South generally, Jim Crow had barely been disturbed, despite a host of federal court orders banning segregation.

Nonetheless, the success of the sit-ins had placed nonviolent direct action at the cutting edge of the black struggle, setting off an intense competition for the strategic initiative among established civil rights organizations. Leaders concluded that only direct federal intervention would overcome the organized resistance of white Southerners, and that a sustained, well-publicized, and severe conflict with local authorities in the deep South would provoke the desired federal reaction. The first to act on this premise was CORE.

James Farmer, just returned to CORE as national director, announced a plan in March 1961 to revive the Journey of Reconciliation under the rubric "Freedom Rides." The goal was to secure enforcement of a 1960 Supreme Court decision banning segregation in waiting rooms, rest rooms, coffee shops, and other facilities serving interstate travellers. Farmer was also determined to test an aspect of Gandhian technique which the CORE pioneers had prudently deferred in the 1940s.

"We felt that one of the weaknesses of the student sit-in movement had been that as soon as arrested, the kids bailed out. . . This was not quite Gandhian and not the best tactic. A better tactic would be to remain in jail and make maintenance of segregation so expensive for the state and city that they could no longer afford it. Fill up the jails, as Gandhi did in India, fill them to bursting if we had to."

SNCC's student leaders, who had reached the same conclusion independently, termed it "jail, no bail." It would become a tactical mainstay of the civil rights struggle.

Thirteen Freedom Riders—seven black and six white—departed Washington, D.C. by bus on May 4, destined for New Orleans. At each rest stop they deliberately violated the code of segregation. "For Colored" and

**A Greyhound bus carrying freedom riders is burned outside Anniston, Alabama, May 1961.**

## 28

"For White" signs had been hastily removed from stations in the upper South, and the journey was relatively peaceful until they reached northern Alabama. Outside Anniston, one bus was halted by gunfire and burned to a shell. Another bus continued to Birmingham, where a white mob, wielding baseball bats and pipes, attacked the Freedom Riders. The police were nowhere in sight; they had promised not to interfere for 15 minutes.

Unable to convince any bus driver to take them further, the group abandoned the trip, but 10 Nashville students sped to Birmingham vowing to resume the journey. With the violence in Alabama front page news across the country, Attorney General Robert Kennedy intervened, demanding that Greyhound provide a bus and ordering Governor John Patterson to provide police protection.

The new group of Freedom Riders set out for Montgomery on May 20 accompanied by 16 highway patrol cars and one state airplane. The escort disappeared on the outskirts of Montgomery and upon arrival at the bus station the Freedom Riders were attacked again. The following night, a riotous white mob surrounded a community meeting at the First Baptist Church and held a thousand blacks hostage inside; federal marshalls repulsed an attempt to storm the church. Governor Patterson finally declared martial law and mobilized 800 national guardsmen to restore order.

CORE, SNCC, and SCLC now agreed that the Freedom Rides should continue. A group of 12 departed for Jackson, Mississippi, where they were promptly arrested for attempting to use a white rest room. They refused to pay fines and were sent to the state prison farm. Though Robert Kennedy appealed for a cooling-off period, by the end of the summer over 300 Freedom Riders—more than half of them college students—had served time in Mississippi jails.

On September 22, the Interstate Commerce Commission handed the protestors a victory with an order banning segregated facilities in bus and train stations. In a broader sense, too, the Freedom Rides affirmed the strategic premises of CORE and SNCC. A sustained Gandhian protest had seized the attention of the nation, exposing millions of Americans to a spectacle of white mob violence and official complicity. This, in turn, forced high federal officials to intervene in a decisive fashion.

But the sit-ins and Freedom Rides were the work of a relatively small, mobile cadre of students and professional activists. SNCC, in particular, felt the need to develop indigenous leadership and a broader base for direct action in the black communities of the South. Albany, Georgia, became the testing ground for that objective.

**The spectre of white mob violence compelled the federal government to insist on protection for the freedom riders. Below, Alabama National Guardsmen and Highway Patrolmen on escort duty.**

29

## Southern Battlefields
# Albany and Birmingham

Twenty-two year-old Charles Sherrod and eighteen year-old Cordell Reagon—sit-in veterans who had left college to become full-time SNCC organizers—arrived in Albany, Georgia, in October 1961. A city of 60,000, forty percent black, Albany had experienced little racial conflict; Sherrod recalls an atmosphere of fear and resignation. He and Reagon organized nightly workshops on nonviolence for the city's black youth, buttonholing prospects in churches, social meetings, pool halls, lunch rooms, and night clubs.

On November 1, effective date of the Interstate Commerce Commission ruling, the young people opened a campaign to desegregate the local bus station. Although they chose not to be arrested on that occasion they were joined in succeeding weeks by flying squads of SNCC activists who arrived via bus from Atlanta, attempted to use the "white" facilities, and were promptly jailed.

The demonstrations were a catalyst for the adult leaders of the black community. They formed a broad coalition known as the Albany Movement, headed by William G. Anderson, an osteopath, and Slater King, a realtor. The coalition organized a series of rallies and marches, increasingly large and militant, which culminated in the December 16 arrest of Martin Luther King, Jr. and 250 of his followers at a "prayer march" en route to City Hall.

King had not planned to be arrested. He had come to town for a one-night appearance at the invitation of the Albany Movement, but the indigenous spirit of the campaign drew him into the struggle. He announced that he would spend Christmas in jail. Later he agreed to bail out, accepting the City's promise to comply with the ICC order in return for a temporary moratorium on demonstrations. The settlement became a national embarrassment for King when Albany reneged on its commitments.

Protest continued through the winter and spring of 1962 with declining momentum and minimal results. A selective boycott of retail businesses was 50 to 75 percent effective but not crippling; a bus boycott patterned on Montgomery forced the line into bankruptcy rather than desegregation. Broadened to attack all forms of segregation in Albany, the campaign lacked a clear focus.

The tempo of the movement revived in the summer when King returned for sentencing on the December charges. A late July march ended in a clash between rock-throwing youths and police, bringing the national guard to Albany. During one week in August, 1000 protestors went to jail. Among those arrested during this period were some 70 ministers, many of them white, whom King had invited from around the country as "witnesses" to the struggle. But Albany Police Chief Laurie Pritchett defused the impact of the protests by minimizing vigilante and police violence, protecting King from attack, and

**Police chief Laurie Pritchett waits while six blacks kneel in prayer on the steps of Albany City Hall, July 1962.**

**Chanting "Freedom, Freedom," members of the Albany Movement wave papers pledging them to risk arrest by marching the following day.**

farming out prisoners to jails in adjacent counties. As SNCC worker Bill Hansen observed, "We ran out of people before he ran out of jails." The City held firm and the movement dissipated.

The national press interpreted Albany as a crushing defeat for King, SCLC, and the civil rights movement. Many insiders shared this assessment and attributed it to poor strategic coordination and the "constant war," as Sherrod called it, between SNCC and SCLC. SNCC organizers were deeply committed to developing new, indigenous leaders and putting them in front-line roles. While recognizing the value of King's prestige to the Albany campaign, they resented SCLC's monopoly of press coverage and outside funds. And unlike King, whom they sarcastically referred to as "Da Lawd," the SNCC activists were reluctant to condemn the angry vandalism of local youths. The unyielding resistance of white Albany had shaken their commitment to nonviolent tactics.

Yet in retrospect it is clear that Albany was a strategic breakthrough. It was the first major campaign to combine the sustained mass participation of the Montgomery bus boycott with the direct action militancy of the sit-ins and Freedom Rides. It was the prototype for the climactic series of civil rights protests: directed by broad-based local coalitions, backed by national organizations, aimed at all forms of segregation, and employing every known direct action tactic from the boycott to the prayer vigil. Even many of the "freedom songs" which were the anthems of the movement could trace their origins to the Albany struggle and its fusion of sophisticated activism with black folk culture.

The most decisive of the Albany-style campaigns unfolded in Birmingham, Alabama, during the summer of 1963. In this instance, the involvement of King and his

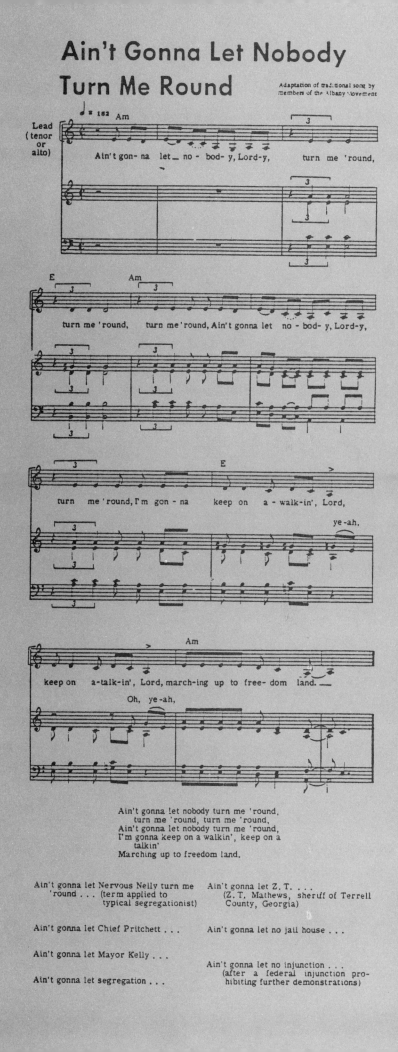

# Ain't Gonna Let Nobody Turn Me Round

Adaptation of traditional song by members of the Albany Movement

Ain't gonna let nobody turn me 'round,
    turn me 'round, turn me 'round,
Ain't gonna let nobody turn me 'round,
I'm gonna keep on a walkin', keep on a
    talkin'
Marching up to freedom land.

Ain't gonna let Nervous Nelly turn me 'round . . . (term applied to typical segregationist)

Ain't gonna let Chief Pritchett . . .

Ain't gonna let Mayor Kelly . . .

Ain't gonna let segregation . . .

Ain't gonna let Z. T. . . . (Z. T. Mathews, sheriff of Terrell County, Georgia)

Ain't gonna let no jail house . . .

Ain't gonna let no injunction . . . (after a federal injunction prohibiting further demonstrations)

Birmingham, May 1963: Police dogs and firehoses failed to quell mass demonstrations.

aides was sought from the outset by the local SCLC affiliate. "They needed us," recalls Rev. Ed Gardner, a Birmingham leader, "and we needed them."

The Birmingham movement needed King because seven years of organized protest, studiously ignored by the local media, had failed to dent Jim Crow. As a national figure, King would at the very least attract outside coverage and seize the attention of the white community.

For King and his aides, Birmingham was a logical focus for the regional struggle against segregation, an ideal locale to redeem the failures of Albany. The most segregated large city in the country, it was notorious for house bombings and other violent acts against blacks. Public Safety Commissioner Eugene "Bull" Connor had built his political career on an unyielding commitment to white supremacy. There was reason to expect that Connor's response to direct action protests would lack the subtlety and restraint of Albany's Laurie Pritchett.

After demonstrations began in early April, the Birmingham authorities obtained a court injunction against

marching. King chose to ignore it and was arrested. The demonstrations continued unabated, with thousands of protestors—among them hundreds of school children—going to jail. In early May, Bull Connor's restraint collapsed and his officers attacked demonstrators on several occasions with unleashed police dogs, billy clubs, and pressurized water from fire hoses.

The ferocity of these attacks forced the Kennedy Administration to act. Administration officials directed an intensive lobbying campaign at Birmingham's civic leaders, with veiled threats of military intervention. Shaken by five weeks of mounting disorder, the businessmen had little heart to resist. They agreed to desegregate downtown stores and hire black sales workers in exchange for a halt to the demonstrations.

In the ten weeks following the Birmingham settlement, more than 750 civil rights demonstrations erupted in 186 Southern communities; nearly 15,000 protestors were arrested. On June 11, President Kennedy appeared on national television to urge Congressional passage of an Administration bill prohibiting racial discrimination in public accommodations. The bill was a substitute for a much weaker measure which the Administration had submitted in February. In private conversations with civil rights leaders, the President admitted that the street protests had forced his hand.

"The big thing was when we had the final demonstration that tied up the whole city . . . This brought the power structure in. See, they had tried to play it as though nothing was happening, but when we marched downtown . . . marched in every department store, every eating joing, and tied up everything, all the traffic, everything was at a standstill.

We had forty-five hundred folks in jail, and we had about ten or twenty thousand wanted to get in, and Bull Connor had filled up the Bessemer jail, had filled up the county jail . . . and when he ran out of space, he got the firemen and turned the water on, but the more water he would pour, the more they would come. So then the power structure said something had to be done.

I remember one man, Sid Smyer. Sid Smyer said, 'I'm a segregationist from bottom to top, but gentlemen, you see what's happening.' He said, 'I'm not a damn fool' . . . Said, 'We can't win. We gon' have to stop and talk to these folks.'"

Rev. Ed Gardner
Birmingham SCLC

**The proliferation of demonstrations across the South repeatedly forced the U.S. Justice Department to intervene. Below, Assistant Attorney General Nicholas Katzenbach charts the progress of desegregation.**

## "One Man, One Vote"

To demonstrate the depth and breadth of support for federal civil rights legislation, movement strategists revived A. Philip Randolph's old idea of a March on Washington. The August 23 event succeeded beyond its organizers' dreams. Endorsed by an impressive array of respectable allies, from the United Auto Workers union to the National Council of Churches, and backed by the entire gamut of civil rights organizations, it attracted a peaceful, well-integrated legion of 250,000—more than any previous demonstration in U.S. history.

Martin Luther King, Jr. captured the buoyant optimism of the occasion in his celebrated address to the marchers, "I Have a Dream." But SNCC chairman John Lewis delivered a more critical appraisal of the pending civil rights act and the progress of the movement. "We have nothing to be proud of," Lewis declared. He cited the bill's failure to address economic inequality, to protect civil rights workers from police dogs and fire hoses, or to guarantee voting rights for blacks. Decrying those who counseled patience, Lewis urged the continuation of the "great social revolution sweeping our nation" and issued a call which would soon dominate the movement, "One man, one vote."

Voting rights, a longstanding issue for Southern blacks, had been overshadowed in the previous decade by the struggle to integrate schools and public facilities. Ironically, its renewed prominence could be traced to Kennedy Adminstration efforts to defuse the political impact of the civil rights movement.

As a Democrat, the President was keenly sensitive to the distance between his party's Northern and Southern wings. Each successive protest exacerbated this tension by spurring demands for action from Northern Democrats, demands which could not be satisfied without alienating Southern voters and key Southern Congressmen whose support Kennedy needed on other issues.

Administration strategists reasoned that the exercise of black voting rights would provoke a less violent response from white Southerners than desegregation, and that an increased black vote would compensate for the defection of hard-line segregationists. After the Administration's first civil rights crisis—the 1961 Freedom Rides—they urged black activists to channel their energies into voter registration in the Deep South. The proposal was sweetened by promises of federal cooperation and access to large grants from liberal foundations.

Within SNCC the offer provoked heated debate. Some derided it as an attempt to blunt the movement. Others maintained that voting was a necessary tool in the struggle and that, contrary to the Adminstration's assumptions, a mass voter registration effort in the deep South would provoke a vehement response from white racists. This argument proved compelling to a number of SNCC activists, who in July 1961 opened a voter registration project in Mississippi, where barely two percent of blacks were registered.

While SNCC was the prime mover, other civil rights groups participated in the Mississippi mobilization. They

**Instead of mounting demonstrations, SNCC organizers in Mississippi went door-to-door encouraging residents to register and vote. Project director Robert Moses: "You organize pound by pound, small bands of people. You create a small striking force capable of moving out when the time comes."**

**Leading the August 1963 March on Washington are (left to right) Whitney Young of the Urban League, Roy Wilkins of the NAACP, A. Philip Randolph, Walter Reuther of the United Auto Workers, and Arnold Aaronsen of the National Jewish Community Relations Council.**

35

36

formed an umbrella organization known as the Council of Federated Organizations (COFO), directed by Robert Moses, a Harlem-born and Harvard-educated SNCC field secretary, with CORE's David Dennis as his assistant, and Aaron Henry of the Mississippi NAACP as president.

Under Moses' leadership, SNCC concentrated its voter registration efforts in the black-majority counties of the Mississippi Delta. Even more than the Albany movement, the Mississippi campaign reflected SNCC's unique commitment to take the civil rights movement beyond its urban, middle-class origins. Moses emphasized the development of indigenous leadership and virtually all his staff members were locally recruited. In place of dramatic, direct action protests, SNCC organizers went from door to door "talking to people about what they're interested in." According to organizer Lawrence Guyot, "If it was fishing, how do you turn that conversation into 'when you gonna register to vote?' If it was religion—that was easier to turn into registering. If it was cotton acreage— our basic verbal mien was that there's nothing that's not involved with politics."

This patient, cautious approach did not insulate the voter registration project from intimidation and violence. Herbert Lee, a farmer who was one of the first local activists, was shot and killed by a white state legislator. On the day she registered to vote, Fannie Lou Hamer's family was evicted from the plantation they had sharecropped for

"See, the simplicity of the political apparatus in Greenwood was made much clearer than if our enemies would have simply said, 'All right, we're not gonna cut off the food. We're not gonna fire people. We're even gonna register a couple. We'll register ten percent of the ones y'all bring down.' But more and more, the black people would see that the board of supervisors controlled everything. What they didn't control they left to the chief of police. It's easy to sell political involvement when you have that kind of activity by an identifiable political apparatus."

Lawrence Guyot

**Two of the 150 blacks who attempted to register on "Freedom Day" in Hattiesburg, MS.**

37

38

Denied the right to register, Mississippi blacks organized a symbolic election in November 1963 to demonstrate their determination to vote. Above, in Belzoni, SNCC established a street corner polling place to collect "freedom ballots" Right, a poster urges support for the freedom ticket.

18 years. County officials in Leflore halted distribution of federal surplus foods. Despite repeated appeals, the Kennedy Administration failed to deliver on its promise of federal protection.

"We really couldn't tell people that we had a way of protecting them," field secretary Charles Cobb recalls. "So, given that reality, our decision was basically just to be physically present in the county, just to show people . . . that we were prepared to stay and stick it out."

At the time of the March on Washington, fewer than 4000 new black voters had registered in Mississippi. Moses realized that his homegrown movement could not succeed without national intervention and that new strategies were needed to bring this about. His central idea was to create a parallel electoral apparatus through which blacks could demonstrate their desire to vote.

In November 1963, COFO set up its own polling places and nominated its own "Freedom" candidates: Aaron Henry for governor and Ed King, a white college chaplain, for Lieutenant Governor. With the aid of a hundred white student volunteers from the North, some 80,000 blacks—nearly a quarter of those eligible—turned out to vote in the symbolic election.

Encouraged by the results, Moses proposed an ambitious plan to bring hundreds of students to Mississippi the following summer. The students would conduct conventional voter registration drives while also enrolling blacks in a "Freedom Democratic Party" designed to challenge the official state delegation to the 1964 Democratic

National Convention in Atlantic City. Moses calculated that an influx of white students would provide publicity and a measure of protection to the campaign.

"We knew that if we had brought in a thousand blacks, the country would have watched them slaughtered without doing anything about it," Dave Dennis explains. "If there were gonna take some deaths to do it, the death of a white college student would bring on more attention to what was going on than for a black college student getting it. That's cold, but that was also. . . speaking the language of this country."

While most of the 700 volunteers were still in training sessions up North, three civil rights workers, two of them white, disappeared near Philadelphia, Mississippi. President Lyndon Johnson, Kennedy's successor, dispatched hundreds of FBI agents and U.S. Navy personnel to find the bodies, which were uncovered after a six-week search. Although the incident created a national furor, it did not measurably alter the federal government's "hands-off" stance on voter registration.

Only 1600 voters had been added to the official registration rolls at the end of "Freedom Summer." But more than 80,000 had registered with the Mississippi Freedom Democratic Party (MFDP). Barred from participating in the regular state party activities, MFDP members held their own conclave and elected 68 delegates to the Democratic National Convention.

The MFDP delegates arrived in Atlantic City with high hopes of unseating the all-white Mississippi regu-

"One great thing I think was introduced in the South with reference to SNCC's tactics was the business of organizing leadership. If 'leven people went to jail this evening who the power structure considered leaders, tomorrow morning you had 'leven more out there. And the next morning 'leven more."

Amzie Moore
President, COFO

**Fannie Lou Hamer became a vice-chair of the Mississippi Freedom Democratic Party and its candidate for Congress.**

lars. They were equipped with strong arguments. The regulars were not only vulnerable on civil rights, they were suspect on party loyalty, having openly threatened to desert Lyndon Johnson for Republican presidential candidate Barry Goldwater. Black Democrats and influential white allies like UAW President Walter Reuther and attorney Joseph Rauh lobbied convention delegates on behalf of the MFDP challenge.

Johnson, however, was not swayed. Fearing the loss of Southern votes, he wielded his immense influence as the incumbent to erode delegate support for the challenge. He remained adamant even after Fannie Lou Hamer's televised testimony before the Credentials Committee—a dramatic account of her eviction, jailing, and beating for attempting to vote—produced a deluge of telegrams from supportive Democrats. All Johnson would offer the MFDP was two at-large delegate seats and a promise to eliminate discrimination at future conventions.

As pressure from the top intensified, key white allies defected. National civil rights leaders Bayard Rustin and Martin Luther King, Jr. urged acceptance of Johnson's deal as a "moral victory." Hamer retorted, "What do you mean moral victory? We ain't getting nothing." Mississippi blacks hadn't risked death, she said, for a token two seats. After hours of tense debate, the MFDP delegates flatly rejected the compromise. Using borrowed passes, they invaded the convention floor to press their case, interrupting convention business for several tumultous hours.

This final, futile demonstration reflected the disillu-

## Freedom Schools

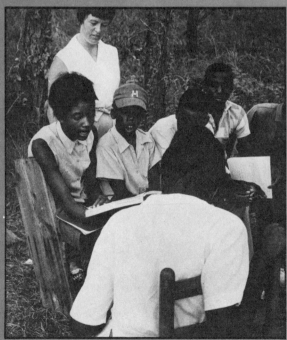

Beyond its immediate political objectives, the 1964 Mississippi summer project aimed to build a cadre of young activists who would carry on the struggle once the Northern volunteers were gone. To do so, SNCC organizers conceived an innovative "Freedom School" program, whose overriding purpose was to help students "begin to question."

A standard curriculum included regular academic subjects but emphasized discussion of black history and culture, the power structure, and the movement. Project planners expected to draw 1000 high school students. By summer's end, more than 3000—some as young as nine and some grandmothers in their 70's—had attended 50 make-shift schools set up in churches, storefronts, sheds, and open fields.

The Freedom Schools were SNCC's first attempt to replace existing institutions with black-controlled alternatives, and they served as a model for the "free school movement" which emerged later in the decade.

sionment of the Mississippi activists. SNCC field secretary Stokely Carmichael observed that the defeat showed "not merely that the national conscience was unreliable but that, very specifically, black people in Mississippi and throughout this country could not rely on their so-called allies. Many labor, liberal, and civil rights leaders deserted the MFDP because of closer ties to the national Democratic Party."

After Atlantic City, the national civil rights coalition—an uneasy alliance of grassroots activists, established black leaders, liberal notables, and politicians—began to unravel. But it survived long enough to mount a climactic campaign for black voting rights.

SCLC organized a wave of voting rights protests around Selma, Alabama, in early 1965. After a young demonstrator was murdered, Martin Luther King, Jr. called a mass march from Selma to Montgomery, the state capital. As the 500 marchers crossed the Edmund Pettis bridge on March 7, mounted state troopers and local deputies attacked them with tear gas and nightsticks and drove them back to the staging ground at the Brown's Chapel Church.

King vowed to continue the march and thousands of Northern supporters flocked to join him, including such celebrities as Paul Newman, Sammy Davis, Jr., and Marlon Brando. Faced with a crisis on the order of Birmingham and the Freedom Rides, President Johnson delivered the response which the Mississippi activists had sought a few years before. In a televised address, the President asked Congress for legislation permitting federal registrars to intervene in counties where blacks had been denied the right to vote.

Under the protection of federal troops, the Selma-Montgomery march was resumed, drawing 30,000 persons by the time it reached the Alabama capital on March 26. Less than five months later, the landmark Voting Rights Act was signed into law.

**Selma-Montgomery march, 1965.**

42

43

Atlantic City challenge, 1964: MFDP partisans sit down on the boardwalk outside the Democratic National Convention. Below, a lobbying report assesses support among convention delegates.

HAWAII - St. Lo Hotel
  Rep. Thomas Gill
  Sen. Inouye
  Spark Matsunaga - will be willing to see someone from MFDP at the Convention
  Gov. John Burns -

ILLINOIS - Hotels: Continental, Madison, Sorrento, Traymore
  H.G. FIELDS - Credentials Committee
  Mrs. R. Ryan - Credentials Committee
  Jerome M. Ziegler - answered Guyot mailing and said he would support FDP
  Jane Enger - friendly

INDIANA - Hotels: Morton, Seaside
  Miss Josephine Cook - Cred. Comm.
  Hon. R. Vance Hartke - Cred. Comm.
  Mr. Milton Maidenberg - offered to help us at Convention; contact at Morton Hote

MAINE - Malibu Hotel
  Edward S. Muskie - might be a contact

MARYLAND - Marlborough-Blenheim
  Royce Hanson - will vote for us according to Rabbi Bleich

MISSOURI - Traymore
  Harold Gibbons - teamsters; good contact

NEW MEXICO - Deauville
  Henry Kiker, Jr., - lawyer likely to be in our favor
  Mrs. Victor Goetz - friendly to the challenge

OHIO - Seaside-Terrace
  Charles Carney - possible contact

SOUTH DAKOTA - Abbey
  Larry Murel - aid to Sen. McGovern; seems friendly; should be contacted

44

## The Crisis of Victory

"There is no more civil rights movement," concluded SCLC staffer James Bevel in 1965. "President Johnson signed it out of existence when he signed the Voting Rights Act."

Bevel recognized that the movement had attained its preeminent goals; in less than a decade, it had demolished the legal edifice of Jim Crow schools, elections, and public facilities. Yet despite the radical advances in law, the position of ordinary black Americans had scarcely improved. Between 1952 and 1963, black family income had actually declined in relation to white income from 57 to 53 percent. Racial discrimination was still prevalent on the job, on the street, and at City Hall. Although housing discrimination was technically illegal, in practice the majority of blacks were confined to ghetto districts where public and private services were visibly inferior to white neighborhoods.

The racial problem did not evaporate after 1965, and neither did the racial movement—a dynamic configuration of competing national organizations, battle-tested organizers, and an aroused rank and file. But the direction of the movement became the subject of bitter debate.

What A. Philip Randolph called a "crisis of victory"

had its most dramatic impact on the young activists of SNCC and their peers in other civil rights organizations. Many believed that further progress was contingent on a radical transformation of the American social and economic structure, and the MFDP debacle in Atlantic City had convinced them that influential white elements in the civil rights coalition—and more established black elements, for that matter—would not endorse fundamental changes.

Moreover, the massive influx of white students in 1963 and 1964 had raised a different concern, about the tendency of these highly articulate outsiders to overwhelm the indigenous leadership that SNCC had consistently sought to nurture. This tension was sharpened by the growing influence of black nationalist ideologies, popularized by spokesmen like Malcolm X. Even those activists who remained committed to integration agreed on the need for a more assertive racial self-image. Finally, there was a cumulative reaction to white violence; anger was no longer suppressed, and many blacks who had earlier questioned an absolute commitment to nonviolence began to accept armed self-defense as a necessity.

All these currents converged in June 1966 at the "March Against Fear" in Mississippi, the disharmonious grand finale of the civil rights coalition. James Meredith, the first black to enter the University of Mississippi, had

**Stokely Carmichael (background) is arrested in Greenwood, Mississippi, June 16, 1966. In a speech that night, he sounded the controversial cry, "Black Power," which exposed the strategic conflicts fracturing the civil rights coalition.**

**In the mid-1960s, after its sweep across the South, black protest moved North. CORE members block traffic on New York's Triborough Bridge in a protest against school conditions in East Harlem, 1964.**

46

been wounded by a sniper in the course of a quixotic protest walk across the state, and civil rights leaders from Roy Wilkins of the NAACP to Stokely Carmichael of SNCC poured into Mississippi to continue the march.

On June 16, police stopped a group of marchers attempting to pitch tents on the grounds of a black public school, arresting several of them. At a rally that evening, Carmichael declared that he would never willingly be arrested again. "What we gonna start saying now is 'black power!'" he shouted and the crowd shouted the slogan back.

"Black Power" crystallized the latent tensions within the movement. The NAACP immediately condemned the slogan, CORE supported it, while King, anxious to maintain links with the younger activists, would neither endorse nor repudiate it. SNCC espoused it most fervently, expelling whites from the organization in December.

The rhetorical thrust of the Black Power slogan was unmistakable as a calculated affront to complacency and an assertion of racial pride. As a strategic prescription, however, it came to mean vastly different things to different people. For some, pro and con, it was synonymous with armed revolution; for others it was as innocuous as black-owned business enterprises. Even within the electoral arena, where Black Power had its most sustained application, its import was ambiguous.

Organized black voting blocs had flourished in some large cities well before the Voting Rights Act, though as a rule they were closely tied to white-dominated party organizations. In the late 1960's, black voters became more demanding and more autonomous. In some instances, they organized independent parties and independent candidacies to press their demands. While these independent electoral movements failed to endure, they often succeeded in winning concessions from local Democratic Party structures, and the number of elected and appointed black officials soared. But increased electoral presence did not translate into the economic and social gains envisioned by the Black Power strategists.

Another response to the crisis of victory was the escalation of racial protest in the cities of the North and West, which now housed nearly half of the nation's blacks. Desegregation and voting rights, which had a concrete impact on the lives of many black Southerners, had no practical significance in communities were blacks had always voted and Jim Crow was not an issue. The contrast between the heralded civil rights victories and the harsh realities of black American life was particularly acute in the ghetto neighborhoods of the big cities. Major riots erupted in Harlem in 1964 and Los Angeles' Watts neighborhood in 1965, escalating to 21 cities in 1966 and 75 in 1967.

The riots and conditions they dramatized inspired a wave of efforts to organize black communities in the North. Martin Luther King, Jr. moved to Chicago in 1966 and targeted housing segregation. "There are more Negroes in

## 47

"From Protest to Politics": Above, a billboard erected by the Lowndes County Freedom Organization (LFCO), an independent party in Alabama whose symbol was later adopted by the Black Panther Party in California. LFCO championed independent political action and sanctioned armed self-defense. Below, Lucius Amerson campaigns with his family in Macon, County, Alabama. Elected in 1966, he was the first black sheriff in the Deep South since Reconstruction.

## 48

Chicago than in the whole state of Mississippi," he declared, "and if we don't get nonviolent groups, the alternative is Watts." CORE concentrated on job discrimination while SNCC shifted its community organizing focus from the rural South to Atlanta and scattered Northern cities. In 1967, the Black Panthers burst out of the Oakland ghetto with a mixture of revolutionary rhetoric and a more prosaic community organizing program.

None of these highly publicized affairs produced an effective model for organizing in the ghetto. SCLC was stymied in Chicago, SNCC and CORE were moribund by 1968, and the Black Panthers collapsed soon after.

It is true that local and national government offered some concessions to black communities during the late 1960s: the black presence increased in such front-line public agencies as the police force and schools; legislatures enacted fair housing and employment statutes; and the Johnson Administration's War on Poverty provided federal funds for employment, training, education, and social service programs in the ghettos. But rather than being credited to protest campaigns, these concessions were usually attributed to judicial pressure, the growing clout of black voters, and the generalized threat of urban disorder. Ghetto organizers had great difficulty establishing the clear linkage between protest and concession, between action and result, which is essential to sustaining the organizing process.

The civil rights movement lost cohesion, force, and mass participation in the years after 1965. Many theories have been advanced to explain this "decline": the diversion of political energy into conventional electoral activity, white reaction to Black Power rhetoric and black separatism, the integration of the black elite and middle class into the American mainstream. In a sense, however, the question is misguided. The movement had achieved its major goals and had created an environment in which other goals—the expansion of black political representation, for example—could be achieved through more conventional means. Its fragmentation and decline were inevitable. The real problem for strategists was not how to maintain the civil rights movement, but how to channel its momentum in a new direction, towards a movement of the urban black poor.

By 1968, the redirection of black activism into economic protest was well underway. Early in the year, Martin Luther King, Jr. announced a national "Poor People's Campaign" and in April he made his fatal trip to Memphis in support of a sanitation worker's strike. These final gestures highlighted the two most vital offshoots of the civil rights movement. One offshoot—the union organizing efforts of low-wage minority workers—brought new vigor to the labor movement. The other—"welfare rights" organizing among the most impoverished Americans—welded the tactical militance of the black freedom struggle to the techniques of another protest tradition, community organizing.

49

From civil rights to economic rights: Above, striking sanitation workers, members of AFSCME, stage a movement-style march in Memphis in 1968. Below, a mule train heads for "Resurrection City," an encampment in Washington, D.C., which was the focal point of the Poor People's Campaign.

50

# COMMUNITY ORGANIZING

# Protest and the City

Humanity has lived in cities for thousands of years, but the urban form we now take for granted is a modern invention. The separation of commercial districts from residential neighborhoods, the stratification of neighborhoods along class lines, the organization of police forces, sanitation, schools, and other services by public authorities—these did not become standard urban features until the latter part of the 19th century. During the same era the United States transformed itself from an agrarian order to an industrial society, and immense cities bloomed on the American continent.

The new urban pattern spawned a new locus of protest, the working class slum: crowded, squalid, and populated by recent migrants from Europe, Asia, and the rural United States. Although the city offered brighter opportunities than a Southern tenant farm or a European ghetto, it was a harsh and bewildering environment for newcomers, replete with unfamiliar hazards. Many who had grown their own food now had to buy it; many who had built their own housing now had to rent it; many who had worked for themselves now had to sell their labor to others. Power in the city resided not in a few nobles or furnish merchants, but in an impersonal apparatus of distant landlords, employers, financiers, judges, politicians, and bureaucrats.

Yet the anonymity of urban life sheltered political dissent, and its sheer density encouraged collective responses to economic distress. The steady expansion of municipal services sparked controversies over service delivery and distribution while creating new expectations for public action against social ills. These two developments—the concentration of the poor in urban slums and the enlargement of municipal responsibility—laid the groundwork for a distinctive form of protest, which would address neighborhood conditions in counterpoint to the struggle of labor in the workplace.

Initially the distinction betwen labor protest and community protest was hardly visible. During the periodic business depressions of the 19th century, thousands of unemployed workers demonstrated on the streets of New York, Philadelphia, Chicago, and other large cities. Demands for work and cash relief were freely linked with calls for lower rents and food prices to offset depressed wages and high unemployment.

Organized labor in New York City took up the housing issue during the severe depression of 1893, demanding that the mayor and governor halt evictions of the unemployed for non-payment of rent. According to AFL President Samuel Gompers, this action served as a model for the New York labor movement, "followed in practically every succeeding crisis."

In May 1902, Jewish women on the Lower East Side of Manhattan organized a boycott of kosher meat butchers who had declined to pass through lower wholesale prices to their customers. Contemporary newspaper accounts reported that hundreds of women roamed the streets of the neighborhood, "screaming and cursing the swindlers of the poor." They forced their way into shops, threw meat on the streets, and doused it with kerosene. Dozens were arrested, fined, or jailed. The boycott was honored by at least 150,000 families on the East Side and spread to Brooklyn, the Bronx, Newark, and Boston.

The Lower East Side also witnessed large-scale rent strikes in the spring of 1904 and in the depression winter of 1907-8, the latter involving some 13,000 protestors. Once again, women took the lead. Bertha Liebson, 19, dubbed "Joan of Arc of the Lower East Side" by *The New York Herald*, was treasurer and chief fundraiser for the 1904 strike organization. Cecilia Arkin, a 16-year-old stenographer, led a fight against her landlord, won a rent

**Eviction on the Lower East Side, early 1900's.**

cut for her building, and became an inspirational symbol of tenant power. Pauline Newman—at age 18 already a veteran of consumer protests against coal and ice merchants—spread the 1907-8 strike uptown to Harlem.

The original female organizers of the East Side rent protests eventually ceded control of the strikes to local Socialist Party activists, predominantly male. It was a characteristic development. Men dominated the parties and trade unions which were the established vehicles of political organization in the slums. The ethos of the time assigned women the task of nurturing home and family and discouraged them from participating in public life. But the working-class woman sometimes violated this code when her domestic responsibilities—spilling into such communal concerns as food, housing and education—sanctioned a spontaneous leadership role in community protest.

Slum residents protest food prices, New York City. Note the line of women leading the rally.

נא, ווערג זיך!

Cartoon from the Yiddish language *Forward*, 1919. The striking women to the baker: "Choke!"

Some affluent, educated women also became committed to improving conditions in the slums. Unwilling to accept the circumscribed role of wife and mother, and excluded from political and professional careers, they turned their attention to the social problems created by the new urban industrial order—particularly its impact on woman, child, and family. "As society grows more complicated it becomes necessary that woman shall extend her sense of responsibility to many things outside of her own home, if only in order to preserve the home in its entirety," argued Jane Addams. In 1889 she founded Hull House, a pioneer "settlement," in the slums of Chicago's West Side.

Others followed her example; by 1900 there were more than 100 settlement houses in the United States, many staffed by women from comfortable backgrounds. The typical settlement provided a range of services to neighborhood residents, from health clinics to playgrounds to English classes, and some went beyond that to promote community improvement efforts and political reforms. Hull House led a neighborhood campaign against inadequate refuse collection, deluging City Hall

A Chicago settlement house organized a brigade of unemployed men to sweep neighborhood streets in a campaign for better sanitation services.

**Children lead a neighborhood march against unsafe tenament housing.**

with 700 complaints in one summer, and attempted to oust the local ward boss from his seat on the Chicago Board of Aldermen. Settlement houses on New York's Lower East Side organized a successful protest against construction of an elevated railroad through the neighborhood. Other settlements campaigned for public playgrounds and baths, child welfare clinics, stricter housing codes, and pure food regulation.

By comparison with the militant labor struggles, food boycotts, and rent strikes of the era, the tactics of the settlement house activists were polite. They relied heavily on skillful manipulation of the press and the exposure of scandals to embarrass political leaders into action. Their campaigns rarely generated mass participation by neighborhood residents, and radicals accused them of treating the symptoms rather than the root causes of slum conditions. But these genteel reformers shaped the development of community organizing in two important ways: by legitimating a new set of public issues, centered in the neighborhoods and at City Hall, and by defining a new vocation known as "social work," which took the improvement of urban slums as its charge.

As municipal governments assumed many of the service functions pioneered by the settlement houses, social work lost much of its reform impetus and placed increasing emphasis on individual "adjustment" to social conditions. But strikes, boycotts, and other forms of community protest continued to be endemic in the larger cities through World War I. A wave of Socialist-led rent strikes in New York City between 1917 and 1920 impelled the Democrats and Republicans to establish their own tenant organizations and speeded the passage of state rent control legislation.

Protest declined during the '20s, then erupted again in the years of the Great Depression. In New York and Chicago, thousands turned out on frequent occasions to resist the eviction of unemployed tenants by marshals and police. These "rent riots" often ended in beatings and arrests. At one such action in the Bronx, *The New York Times* reported, "Women shrieked from windows, the different sections of the crowd hissed and booed and shouted invectives. The marshal's men were rushed on the stairs and got to work after the policemen had driven the tenants back into their apartments."

**Queens, 1936: Expecting eviction, homeowner J. Charles Lane places the deed to his Sunnyside house in a coffin and holds a "wake" and mock funeral for the dead deed.**

As the Depression deepened, the focus of protest shifted to cash relief; spontaneous demonstrations grew larger, more frequent, and better organized. In Chicago, Unemployed Councils mounted 566 demonstrations in 1932, including simultaneous actions at all the relief stations in the city. The protests succeeded in expanding local and federal relief programs and each success fueled more widespread disruption.

Mobs of unemployed in Colorado rioted at relief offices, looted food stores, and took over the state legisla-

8

**A "Hunger March" organized by the Unemployed Councils, Chicago, 1932.**

ture in 1934 to secure state participation in the federal emergency relief program. Two thousand staged a vigil at a Kansas City courthouse until cutbacks in relief funding were restored. Leaders of the unemployed movement formed a nationwide organization—the Workers Alliance of America—which by the end of 1936 claimed 160 locals with a membership of 600,000 in 43 states.

The turmoil of the 1930s affected Americans at every level of society, shaking their loyalties to established ideas and institutions. "In the crisis life became polarized," wrote Saul Alinsky, who was then a young social worker in Chicago. Out of the flux of his experiences in that tumultous era, Alinsky refined a new conception of social action which would permanently alter the course of community protest.

The polarization of "haves" and "have-nots" which Alinsky welcomed in the Depression years did not abolish conflict among the "have-nots." When Alinsky began working in Chicago's Back of the Yards neighborhood in 1938 under the auspices of a metropolitan social agency, he found a community that was almost uniformly working-class yet deeply fragmented.

Located in the stockyards district immortalized by Upton Sinclair's muckraking novel, *The Jungle*, Back of the Yards epitomized the nation's worst slums. With 90,000 residents, primarily Catholics of Eastern European descent, the neighborhood was saturated with churches and social organizations, but these were organized strictly along ethnic lines. The schisms reflected Old World enmities, reinforced by the employers' historic practice of pitting nationalities against each other.

A CIO-affiliated local had made headway in overcoming ethnic animosities at the stockyards and packinghouses, but the union's Communist leadership was anathema to the Church. Thus it was a momentous event when Catholic Bishop Bernard J. Shiel and CIO President John L. Lewis appeared together on July, 16, 1939, at a strike rally in the neighborhood. *Time* magazine described the episode as making "not only Chicago but U.S. history." It symbolized the tentative reconciliation of Church and labor, the triumph of class unity over cultural division, which Alinsky's pioneering efforts had produced in Back of the Yards.

Alinksy's novel organizing philosophy was a synthesis of the social work tradition and militant CIO unionism. His idea for a People's Organization was "in its simplest sense. . . the extension of the principles and practice of organized collective bargaining beyond the confines of the factory gate." Like a labor union, a People's Organization would demand rights rather than begging favors, using conflict to achieve its goals. But it would transcend the narrow focus on wages and hours which Alinsky characterized as the chief failing of the labor movement. "It is ironic," he wrote, "that the same American workingman who recognizes that only through organization. . . can he better his working conditions, does not carry on with organization in dealing with all other problems."

He was harsher in his criticism of social workers, who "come to the people of the slums. . . to get them adjusted to the environment so they will live in hell and like it too." The job of the community organizer, as Alinsky conceived it, was to help slum dwellers rebel. But the organizer did resemble the social worker as a self-conscious professional who was distinct from the body of the community. His role was not to lead rebellion, but to identify and nurture rebellious "native leaders."

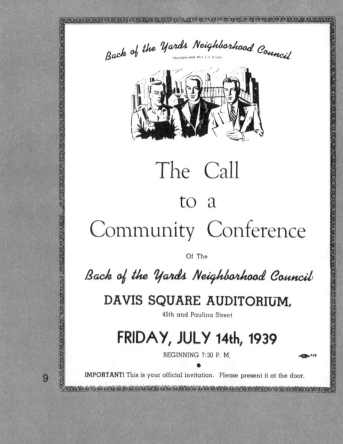

**Saul Alinsky recruited representatives from business, labor, and ethnic churches to make up the founding board of his first "People's Organization".**

Alinsky's sponsors had instructed him to concentrate his work in Back of the Yards on a single issue, juvenile delinquency. He rejected this plan and recruited a local school teacher, Joseph Meegan, to recruit organizations to a neighborhood council with working committees on housing, employment, health, and child welfare. The two men appealed to prospective members on the basis of shared self-interest. As Alinsky later described the process, he convinced church leaders to collaborate with the union not by resorting to moral arguments, but by linking the churches' welfare with their parishioners' financial capacity to contribute to the Sunday collection. Similarly, he urged local businessmen to recognize their dependence on the workers' purchasing power.

By July 14, 1939, they had signed up 50 religious, social, labor, and business groups which sent 350 delegates to the founding congress of the new "organization of organizations," the Back of the Yards Neighborhood Council. It was coincidental that the event occurred on Bastille Day, the French revolutionary anniversary, but the date's connotations were not lost on the founders. The Council adopted as its slogan, "We the People will work out our own destiny."

Discussion was so vigorous that the Congress lasted until two in the morning, much to Alinsky's satisfaction. His interest in democratic process was greater than his commitment to any specific program. While the unions measured their success in wages and hours, the social workers sought policy reforms, and the Communists offered a comprehensive vision of a reconstructed society, Alinsky viewed programmatic issues less as ends than as means to his paramount goal: building an organization capable of contesting for power.

In practice, few of the issues addressed by the council were as controversial as the labor dispute in the packinghouses which occasioned the historic meeting of Lewis and Bishop Shiel two days after the founding congress. Converting vacant lots into playgrounds was far more typical. But every issue, according to Alinsky, is controversial by definition, and even the most mundane controversy offers the radicalizing experience of participation and conflict. "While (people) may accept the idea that organization means power," he later wrote, "they have to experience this idea in action."

By 1941, Alinsky could list 17 accomplishments of the Back of the Yards Neighborhood Council, including construction of a recreation center, securing 2800 jobs through the National Youth Administration and private industry, establishing a credit union, and extending the federal school lunch program. Seeing his theories validated, Alinsky established the Industrial Areas Foundation (IAF) and organized similar stockyard neighborhoods in Kansas City and St. Paul. In 1947 he helped to found an organization in Southern California which would contribute new techniques and insights to the nascent art of community organizing.

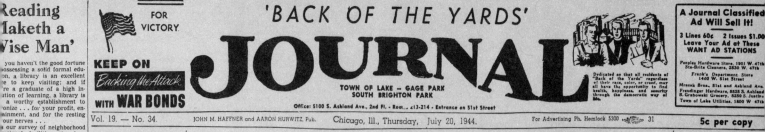

FOR VICTORY

KEEP ON
Backing the Attack
WITH WAR BONDS

'BACK OF THE YARDS'

# JOURNAL

TOWN OF LAKE — GAGE PARK
SOUTH BRIGHTON PARK

Office: 5100 S. Ashland Ave., 2nd Fl. - Room 213-214 - Entrance on 51st Street

Dedicated so that all residents of "Back of the Yards" regardless of their race, color, or creed, may all have the opportunity to find health, happiness, and security through the democratic way of life.



Vol. 19. — No. 34. JOHN M. HAFFNER and AARON HURWITZ, Pub. Chicago, Ill., Thursday, July 20, 1944. For Advertising Ph. Hemlock 5300 31 5c per copy

## 'Reading Maketh a Wise Man'

you haven't the good fortune possessing a solid formal edu- on, a library is an excellent e to keep visiting; and if 're a graduate of a high in- ution of learning, a library is a worthy establishment to onize . . . for your profit, en- ainment, and for the resting our nerves . . .

our survey of neighborhood cational facilities, the four lic and one parish library t not be overlooked.

### St. Augustine

even thousand volumes of rything imaginable", in the ds of the Rev. Justinian Kug- OFM, are contained in the Augustine church library.

**Hours**

here is no official librarian, the ...ds are kept by the ng w... of the parish. It is to ... public from 3:00 to p... every afternoon, and 7:00 to 9:00 p.m. on Wednes- evening.

**25 Years Old**

ne of the longest established he neighborhood, this library pproximately 25 years old.

### Sherman Park

ublicized as one of the most active branch libraries in Chi- , Sherman park library was ted in its present setting at edge of the park in October,

e spacious, new building, designed inside and out, was result of a ten-year cam- n. The old, pagoda-styled ry had inadequate room for the books and patrons.

**Circulation: 11,910 Volumes**

e popularity of the present ry is testified by its statis- Only last month 368 new ons registered for library . The circulation of books une was 11,910, and "it is tantly increasing," explains Ann Kelly, head librarian.

try persons are on the re- list for Betty Smith's "A Grows in Brooklyn," but Signpost," a psychological , is a close runner-up.

ring the summer months an game is under way for the r and intermediate groups. younger readers meet Tues- at 2:00; the next age group, nesdays at 2:00.

**CYO Classes**

two days a week the CYO onducting summer classes. days and Thursdays. A deal of ... in the Sher... ranch by al orders of ... who are ying in Chicago for the sum-

### Gage Park

one time the Gage park branch was housed in a e residence, but with the ing of the Gage park field- e at 55th and Western, in the library was moved into

day, under librarian Miss nor Doyle, it holds a thriving , particularly with its ger customers this summer.

**Popular Books**

Tree Grows in Brooklyn" by y Smith is the book most in and, as it is in many other ries over the city. "The " by Lloyd Douglas follows ose second.

mong juvenile readers "Las- Come Home" is ...ost lar, and has been s... the e production was shown, s Miss Doyle.

**Foreign ...guage Wor...**

ge ...'s foreign s...elves ain books in Bohemian, Ger- Greek, Italian, Polish, Li- nian, and Spanish. The li- ians here will order books in r languages from the main e downtown.

e city-wide army game is ed in Gage on Friday after- s from 2:00 to 3:00. Twenty- members are working for es.

ge sub-branch library hours 1:00 to 6:00 p.m. on Tues- Thursday, and Saturday; to 9:00 p.m. on Monday, nesday, and Friday.

### Cornell Square

rnell square library is one he oldest in the district— t 30 years.

ss Leona E. Cronin, head li- ian, reports that the June ulation amounted to 3,425. re are 5,385 books in the li- y.

**ies Influence Readers' Tastes**

ke many others Miss Cronin rts that "A Tree Grows in oklyn" is by far the most lar right now. "But there always surges in the res- se to current movies, such Jane Eyre." And Somerset gham's "The Razor's Edge" demand also."

**Servicemen Remembered**

rnell square is engaged in ecting books for servicemen, ch they send to the city head- rters.

ibrary hours are from 1:00 to p.m. on Monday, Tuesday, Thursday, and from 1:00 to p.m. on Wednesday, Friday, Saturday.

e summer reading corps ts every other week at 2:30 e afternoon, Friday, July 21,

## LIST OF WAR DEAD GROWS; 4 LOSE LIVES

The War and Navy departments have announced that four Back of the Yards men have been killed in action, three are wounded, and one is missing. In addition to this week's official toll, another death has been reported by the family of the deceased.

**Francis Heinrich**

A memorial mass will be held for Pvt. Francis J. Heinrich, son of Mr. and Mrs. Roman Heinrich, 1734 W. 47th, Thursday, July 27, 10:00 a.m., in the St. Rose of Lima church, 48th and Ashland.

The twenty-year-old soldier died in the early part of July. His family had previously been notified that he was injured, and under treatment in a Hawaiian hospital.

Heinrich left Gage Park high school to enter the army 15 months ago. He had been overseas for six months.

Besides his parents, he leaves three sisters, Mrs. Grace Kramarski, Mrs. Blanche Kalafut, and Miss Grace Heinrich; and one brother, Pvt. Raymond A. Heinrich.

**Marine Dies**

One of three Chicago marines to be reported dead is Pfc. Theodore Machowicz, son of Mrs. Bernice Machowicz, 4600 S. Richmond.

**European Sector**

From the European area comes notice of the death of Pfc. Chester A. Brzezinski, son of Mrs. Agnes Brzezinski, 4308 S. Mozart.

Another army man to be killed in action in the European theater of war is T/5 Marin L. Baltica, cousin of Mirio Kesich, 920 S. 50th.

**Mediterranean Casualty**

Pvt. Lee J. Carnegie, husband of Mrs. Alfreida I. Carnegie, 5218 S. Laflin, has been killed in the Mediterranean area.

**Wounded Soldiers.**

The wounded are:

Pfc. John J. Stafford, son of Mrs. Emma Stafford, 1137 W. 55th, European area.

T/4 William G. Weber, brother of Mrs. Alice Lehnert, 5336 S. Laflin, European area.

T/5 Thaddeus Rydecki, son of Mrs. Mary Rydecki, 5143 S. Ada, Mediterranean area.

**Lieutenant Missing**

The husband of Mrs. Danza J. Powers, 2nd Lt. John J. Powers, 5410 S. Justine, is missing in the Mediterranean sector.

## Infantryman's Heroism Noted With Medal

Theodore Zabawa

The Combat Infantryman's badge has been awarded to Pfc. Theodore Zabawa, son of Mrs. Antoinette Zabawa, 5152 S. Wolcott.

The citation issued with the badge reads in part as follows: ". . . You carried on bravely and courageously in the face of overwhelming enemy strength, fighting over a terrain which offered the minimum of cover and concealment, in extremely unfavorable weather conditions."

Zabawa is a member of the

## Old Chicago Teems With Young Love

Since today is July 20, to you, family upon family living on Wolcott street, we'd like to tell about a log-cabin-flavored romance that blossomed in early part of the last century and saw fruition in great wedding. For it is in honor of one of the principals in the marriage that your street is named.

One hundred and twenty-one years ago today, Chicago's first Indian agent married a very young daughter of Chicago's first settler. It is reported to be the initial wedding ceremony to take place in Chicago.

The 33-year-old groom was Dr. Alexander Wolcott, and his bride Ellen M. Kinzie, daughter of John Kinzie. John Hamlin, justice of the peace, performed the ceremony.

Leather thongs heavy with Indian wampum, and a trading post decked with soft, russet pelts and sleek furs may well have been the background for the nuptials, for that is how they lived. Mrs. Wolcott was left a widow by the death of her husband seven years later, in 1830.

The date when Wolcott street first received its name is buried with the middle of the 19th century. For a period of thirty years it was known as Lincoln street, but the original Wolcott was restored within the last decade.

And that is the story behind Wolcott street.

Sentiment-minded followers of the pioneer love story will be comforted to know that the Kinzie clan is remembered in a rather obscure, we are sorry, industrial street in the near North side.

No more of the tale is recorded in history books. The rest of the story must come from the imagination of today's children, and from the pens of novelists.

## Draft, in 4th Year, Is Still Going Strong

The following named registrants of Local Board No. 98, 4624 S. Western, were selected to report to the Armed Forces Induction station, July 11.

Frank Walter Przytula, 4601 S. Rockwell; Stanley J. Kolodziejczyk, 4828 S. Wolcott; Florian A. Dlotkowski, 4542 S. Talman; Walter Joseph Glowacz, 4548 S. Talman; Thaddeus F. Witkowski, 4611 S. Kedzie; Bernard Theodore Kumzi, 4062 S. Campbell; Edward Bruno Dober, 4615 S. Rockwell; Stanley Frank Czaja, 4120 S. Richmond; Anthony Frank Zilis, 4424 S. Washtenaw; Anthony Thomas Grossi, 3143 W. Lexington; William Pawlowski, 4750 S. Wood; Joseph Paul Lang, 4521 S. Mozart; Raymond John Lach, 3237 W. 66th; Casimir Louis Trzyna, 4731 S. Wolcott; Jacob Andrew Pavlik, 4725 S. Seeley; Frank Peter Malec, 1658 W. 51st, and William Raymond Petrick, 4747 S. Rockwell.

**His Photograph!**

**Would you like to see your service son's picture smiling out at you from the Journal, and know that he is being seen by readers in 20,000 other Journals?**

**You can have his photograph reproduced for a nominal sum. The larger and clearer a negative, the better the engraving.**

**Think About It!**

### Do You Have Trouble Crawling in Windows?

Another key has taken residence in the Journal community for homeless "Open Sesames".

The new inmate, aristocratically clad in a brass chain and plastic fob with the initial "M", was found on the 47th block on Paulina last week. It was turned in by a Journal news carrier.

### Yards and Lancashire

Mr. and Mrs. James Bagley of Lancashire, England, wish to announce the marriage of their daughter Margaret, June 17, at the Sacred Heart Church to

## KIDS WIN APPLAUSE OF LAWMAKERS

"Mr. Meegan," called a voice from the Democratic Resolutions committee, "will you please send in your delegation for the lunch program?"

**Audience of Famous Personages**

The 200 dignified senators and congressmen that made up the audience in the Stevens hotel room last Tuesday morning, July 18, stirred slightly. They had been listening to delegations all morning, and had heard speeches by noted persons from all over America. What delegation was this, they mused, and were its members of national renown?

**Surprise!**

Then Meegan brought in his "delegation"—five solemn-faced children from the Guardian Angel nursery.

Pandemonium flashed through the room. It was a round twenty minutes until the Democratic dignitaries had finished shaking the five small hands, until the photographers had slung their cameras back over their shoulders, until the reporters had retreated to the make-shift pressroom.

**Hot Lunch Program**

Meegan began:

"This is my delegation, Mr. and Miss America of tomorrow . . . We want to perpetuate an insurance policy that has been begun today, the penny milk and hot lunch program. . . ."

He said what he wanted in ten clipped minutes. Later Meegan commented that the BYNC was not a political group, that it had attempted a hearing before the Republican convention, but had been denied it.

**BYNC Invited by Rep. McCormack**

The invitation to be among the 40 groups who won a hearing before the Democratic resolutions committee came from Representative John McCormack, chairman.

Congressman and Mrs. McCormack, together with Jim Hartley of Boston and the Rev. John Hagan, St. Margaret's church, Boston, were guests of the Rev. A. M. Linkus, pastor of Holy Cross, 46th and Hermitage, Sunday.

The Rev. Hagan celebrated the 8:00 mass which McCormack and Hartley attended. All were guests of the Rev. Linkus in the rectory after services.

## JOURNAL PROPOSES GLORIFIED BUDGET FOR PRIZE-TAKERS

Here's a budget that you might contemplate. You'll like this one even if you usually envision budgets as leering, crafty ogres that waft away all your ice cream soda money.

It's a budget for spending the $25 you may win in next week's Journal drawing. Since the prize purse totals $100, four people will have the opportunity.

Now consider this money-saving plan. Take $18.75 out for a war bond, first of all. That leaves $6.25. Now, to be truthful, once you've bought the war bond we don't, of course, care what you do with this remainder of $6.25. However, just to be sociable, we suggest that you buy anything from a watermelon for the family picnic next Sunday to fancy-labeled cologne.

Have your buff colored coupon on hand. It begins with serial number 50441.

Three consolation prizes were distributed last week to Helen Matel, 5043 S. Paulina, Carolina Omastiak, 4741 S. Hoyne, and Rosie Pilat, 4747 S. Western.

## Dive for Cover; But Bombing Is Show-off Plane

"This is it," flashed into the heads of residents of the 4600 Sacramento block early last Saturday morning, when a roaring Liberator bomber skimmed over the housetops and trees.

Despite the screaming of women and scurrying of children, it wasn't an air raid.

## 'Delegates' to National Convention

Conventioneers found an amusing break in a long series of plank-seeking delegations, when the BYNC's delegates turned out to be five children from the Guardian Angel nursery. Pictured above are Joseph Meegan, Rep. John McCormack, and Rep. Mary Norton, members of Resolutions Committee, with these children, right to left, Nancy Gozanski, Angeline Butz, Winifred Foley, Frankie Wydra, and George Wassik.

Photo Courtesy Chicago Sun

## Our Soldier Sees Vatican, Meets Pope

Among the first American doughboys to shake hands with Pope Pius XII after troops stormed Rome recently was Pfc. Frank J. Marek, Jr., son of Mr. and Mrs. Frank Marek, 3233 S. California.

Twenty-one-year-old Marek entered the army early in 1943. A

Frank J. Marek, Jr.

member of the 88th division, he has been overseas eight months, and was in several major battles of Italy.

To his credit are a small group of German prisoners of war, which he himself captured.

Marek, an only child, graduated from Kelly high, June, 1941. In civilian life he was a welder with the Nechin Iron works.

## Devise New Medical Use for Blood

Did you know these new scientific facts about the blood you give to the Red Cross?

1. The red corpuscles, discarded from the plasma solution given to the wounded, are saving lives among civilians.

Everything from acute arthritis to tuberculosis has been treated with the red cells, and with results as phenomenal as the sulfa drugs.

2. These same red cells have been powered, and used to dust stubborn lesions. "Miraculous healing" has resulted, say doctors.

3. Twenty-five New Englanders who had undergone cranial operations now have a very fine

## Court Finds Life Unembellished

The Monday morning session of the Stockyards court at 47th and Halsted is a panorama of life from which the cloak of glamour has been removed.

As the clock on the wall marks off the minutes before the judge's arrival, the benches fill with a motley assortment of people — dapper lawyers, hastily dressed women whose husbands haven't been home for the last two nights, belligerent landlords and tenants who "know their rights". To some the bleak-walled courtroom is familiar—the usual anticlimax to sorrow. Others are shocked by the very prosaic quality of the room and people in it.

**Husband in Trouble**

"Me ole man is in the lockup agin," confides a faded old woman. "Drunk." Her shabby hat sits rather abruptly on her short, grizzled hair. She waits, brushing her purse nervously with hands that are stiff from scrubbing other people's floors. "How do I know how he will look, spending his nights in the streets and drinking and all?"

Judge N. Bonnelli enters the room and it quiets.

**Plain English**

"Hear ye, hear ye, court is now in session," drones the bailiff as if all the white-wigged pomp of the old English courts surrounded him. Then, for the intelligence of the persons who stare blankly at him, he tops the ritual with a lusty, "Keep quiet!"

**Family Asks Jail for Young Man**

"First case!"

A gaunt—rather young—man is brought from the adjoining cells. His mother, who is standing with another woman, starts when she sees him.

"Judge, this man is my nephew," begins the other woman, whose face is noticeably flushed.

The young man leans forward, clenching the bench. The courtroom is aware of his trembling shoulders. His face is hidden.

"He drinks and we can't stop him. He's not a bad boy, but he just isn't well, and so we'd like to have him put . . ." The aunt breaks down. She turns to the young man. "We don't like to have you go, but it's the best thing for you."

The judge talks, softly and firmly, the aunt answers, but few in the courtroom are watching them. All are looking at the young man's face, now turned ... lined by block brows and hair.

The case is continued.

**Wife-beater?**

"Next!"

Three persons step up, a sad-eyed older woman, her daughter —a militant reproduction of the mother—and a tiny little man, who looks more like a miniature out of a dollhouse than a wife-beater.

After the wife has a brief say in broken English and the daughter a prolonged one in 1944 slang, Judge Bonnelli turns to the defendent, who is grinning inappropriately. "Well, what have you to say?"

"That woman talks lies!" the little man asserts, still grinning sheepishly.

"Well! And do you never tell

(Continued on page 2)

## Council Sets Canteeners Out on Own Wings

A final decision to adopt "Teen Canteen" as its permanent name was reached recently by the high school group that has sponsored dances for the last two weeks in the St. John of God Parish hall, 52nd and Throop.

The fledgling club is the result of the BYNC's attempt to provide entertainment for young persons between 13 and 19. Forwarding it a juke-box and money enough to buy a supply of swing records, the Council has now put the club on its own. The Rev. Edward E. Plawinski will supervise these affairs.

Meeting every Wednesday and Saturday, the dancers generally number 160.

"Beginners may arrive at 7:30 on either night to brush up," advised the Canteeners' president, Edwin Pawlak, 5134 S. Bishop. "But things really get going at 8:00, and last until 11:30."

Until a clubroom of its own can be found, the "Teen Canteen" will remain at St. John of God. Members intend to rent their own hall before fall.

A slight boost in admission has been made to 12c on Wednesday, juke-box night, and 25c on Saturdays, band night. Refreshments are always served.

"We are in the market for bands," added Pawlak, "and will consider any that want to play

## LOSE WIND ON LAST LAP OF BOND RACE

Their position in the entire city line-up dropping slightly since last week, Town of Lake, Garfield-Damen, Sherman Park and Gage Park are now 34th, 39th, 40th and 41st respectively in the "batting averages" of the city's 108 communities.

**Percentages**

The percentages owned by these areas are:

Town of Lake, .326;
Garfield-Damen, .479;
Sherman Park, .475; and
Gage Park, .437.

**Division III**

Division three, of which these four communities form a part is still at the top of the six Chicago divisions with an average of .511, and sales aggregating $27,984,853.

**Gage Park**

Individual community reports are still incomplete. Gage Park announces that 6,930 sales amounting to $620,655, have been made. Red, White, and Blue credit slips total $410,230.25 for the district.

Frank J. Loeffler, commander states: "The community has never tackled a job with so much vigor or determination."

A co-worker, Al Baman, war bond chairman for Gage Park has this to say:

"Now that the Fifth War Bond Drive is nearing a close I want to thank Mrs. Lillian Vondrasek Mr. Milton Kman, Mr. Duckworth, Mr. Doebler, Mr. Rapp and Mr. Payne for the wonderful co-operation they have given me and the community by going into zones other than their own to solicit bonds."

A drive withi... been designated for the week of July 24 by the city OCD for wind-up sales.

**Individual Sales Lag**

Pointing out that bond sales in all categories have been the largest in city and county history, Philip R. Clarke, Chicago chairman, states that sales of bonds to individuals are still short of their $277,000,000 quota.

## Mexican Church Funds Mount After Festival

Clearing of the vacant lot adjoining 4515 S. Ashland, on which the Guadalupe church and social center is to be constructed very soon, climaxed the success of the Mexican festival sponsored July 9 to raise money for the project.

"Thanks for the affair should go first to my parishioners, among them Mrs. Rodriguez, Mr. Chico, Mr. and Mrs. Rangel, Mr. Lopez and the Cardenas school, and the beautiful girls, and Mrs. Flores" stated the Rev. James Tort, C.M.F.

In addition he cited the work of the BYNC, in co-operation with Holy Cross church under the Rev. A. M. Linkus, pastor. Starting with 75 tickets at dollar apiece they finally accumulated over $200.

"I don't know how that happened," mischievously grinned Joseph Meegan, BYNC secretary.

Rev. Tort is now soliciting funds from the Town of Lake merchants. Last week Leo Rose of Leo Rose Credit clothing added $25 to his first check of $100.

"I hope that other business men will respond as Mr. Rose did," added Father Tort.

John S. Reiner of Reiner Coal company has contributed $100. Fifty dollars came from Msgr. Bobal, pastor of SS. Cyril and Methodius.

## Pioneers' Spirits Burn Candles on Annexation Day

Sixty-five spectral birthday candles gleamed on the Town of Lake anniversary cake last Saturday, July 15. Although the festival was imaginary, the occasion was quite real.

In 1889 the Town of Lake along with four other suburbs was annexed to the city of Chicago. This move increased the population by 200,000, and rocketed Chicago to the position of second largest city in the U...

# CSO

Distinguished by language and culture from the Anglo-Americans who conquered the Southwest in the 1840s, California's Mexican-Americans were progressively segregated and disenfranchised in the century following the U.S. conquest. Overt discrimination relegated Chicanos to the lowest-paying work in fields and factories and confined them to isolated "barrios" with inferior housing, schools, and services.

The World War II labor shortage brought a sudden influx of workers from Mexico, crowding the barrios and sharpening animosities between Chicanos and Anglos. After riots erupted in Los Angeles, the Chicago-based American Council on Race Relations sponsored an effort to ease tensions. It hired Fred Ross, who had managed federal farm labor camps during the Depression, to create "councils of civic unity" in Southern California.

Over a pinochle game with the American Council's director, Saul Alinsky heard complaints that, instead of conducting surveys, Ross was "always organizing." His interest piqued, Alinsky arranged a meeting and in September 1947 hired Ross as the IAF's West Coast representative.

Alinsky agreed to finance an organizing project in the barrios but Ross insisted on following his own model. Unlike the Back of the Yards neighborhood with its network of churches, unions, and social groups, the barrios contained few locally controlled institutions, so an "organization of organizations" was not feasible in Ross's view. Instead he proposed to recruit individuals to a "direct membership" organization. And contrary to Alinsky's usual preference for autonomous neighborhood groups, the plan called for a statewide federation.

The first individuals to join the new Community Service Organization (CSO) were veterans of Eduardo Roybal's unsuccessful 1947 campaign for a Los Angeles city council seat. They went door-to-door with Ross in the city's east side slums recruiting more members. To speed this tedious process, Ross devised a new technique, the "house meeting." He asked interested residents to invite a few friends to their homes where, after a discussion of neighborhood problems, he would explain the purpose of CSO, persuade those present to attend the forthcoming chapter formation meeting, and line up commitments to hold additional house gatherings. From one such meeting in San Jose, Ross enlisted Cesar Chavez, a farmworker who soon joined the IAF payroll. As the technique was refined, Ross and Chavez customarily used a six-week series of house meetings to build a solid membership core before convening the first formal chapter meeting.

Ross also introduced a new action strategy to community organizing: mass voter registration. CSO's founders recognized that Roybal's defeat was the consequence of low Chicano turnout, and moreover, that their organization would only wield influence with city officials if it represented organized voters. They engineered a methodical neighborhood canvass, dispatching "bird dogs" to knock on doors and direct residents to street-corner registration tables. By May 1949 they had increased the registration rolls in Los Angeles's ninth councilmanic district from 4000 to 20,000 voters.

Although CSO did not endorse candidates, its get-out-the-vote effort in the ninth district produced an 82 percent turnout—the city's highest—in the 1949 election. Roybal, elected by an overwhelming margin, was the first Chicano councilman in 70 years. And within months of the election the organization could point to scores of new traffic signals and miles of freshly paved roads in the Boyle Heights, Lincoln Heights, and Belvedere neighborhoods.

As CSO expanded to other California communities, voter registration was customarily a new chapter's first activity and often—when local officials balked—its first

13

Fred Ross (right) looks on as Cruz Nevarez, elected chapter president that night, addresses the founding meeting of San Bernadino CSO. Held outside because of hot weather, the meeting capped a six-week membership recruitment drive.

"You see, in most organizations, some fast-talking charm boy gets up and says what needs to be done, and the rest of the people just go ahead and vote for his idea without thinking. So, after awhile, the program becomes his program, not theirs at all, and gradually they drop out and the organization is either dead or ruined. Now, the only way to prevent this in CSO is to start training the people now to quit taking somebody else's word on what's good or bad for them and get them in the habit of always trying to think things out for themselves."

Fred Ross

taste of conflict. In one legendary incident, a county clerk refused to deputize Chicano registrars and the local CSO chapter voted to publicize his conduct. Within twenty minutes, the clerk, who was standing for re-election, had rushed to swear in the prospective deputies.

CSO tactics were not highly demonstrative. Letter-writing campaigns, lawsuits, and appearances at city council were far more common than pickets and marches. But years of deference and isolation lent significance to even the mildest forms of communal assertion, especially since CSO did not shrink from such explosive issues as the conduct of the local police.

Certain police agencies were notorious in the barrios for sidewalk shakedowns, indiscriminate arrests, and brutality. In the Los Angeles "Bloody Christmas" case, where six youths were beaten by police, CSO pressure for disciplinary action sent the attackers to jail. In other instances officers were fined or suspended and police-community friction subsequently declined.

With 37 chapters in 1960, CSO boasted 217,000 newly registered voters, physical improvements in hundreds of neighborhoods, elimination of ethnic segregation in schools and public accommodations, and a "vast reduction" of housing and job discrimination. A less tangible but equally significant product was a new leadership cadre in the barrios. Ross had devoted much of his time and energy to developing indigenous leadership in CSO. He formalized the process in some chapters with a program of weekly "educationals," conducted by grassroots members trained to guide the freewheeling discussion of issues, strategies, and organizing methods.

Dolores Huerta, an educational leader from Stockton, describes the procedure: "You try to crank up your brain. You ask questions to get back to what is basic.

You start with 'what's hurting?' and push on to 'what's wrong?' and 'why?'"

"Your organization is your gun," said another leader, "and you learn in the educational program where to aim it and when to shoot. Another thing you learn. . . is what the shooting is all about."

As intended, the educationals instilled confidence in unschooled members and generated a steady flow of leadership "from the bottom up." But there was a competing source of new leadership: articulate middle-class recruits, attracted by CSO's growing reputation for political clout. Although middle-class members had valuable skills to offer, their methods and priorities were often at odds with the organization's working-class base. Chapters which came under their influence almost invariably shied away from confrontation, relegating discrimination complaints to lawyers while pursuing non-controversial activities such as college scholarship funds.

As the vigor of CSO's advocacy role diminished, so did its membership base. Compounding the difficulty was the organization's grim financial picture. Alinsky, who had raised considerable funds for the California project from foundations and other outside sources, stressed self-sufficiency as the ultimate goal. But unlike an "organization of organizations," which could draw support from its community sponsors, CSO was forced to rely on individual membership dues and special fundraising events. Dues were only two dollars a year and monies raised from picnics and dances were often diverted to popular neighborhood causes like the Cub Scouts.

To stem the membership decline and stabilize finances, Ross proposed to raise dues to twelve dollars a year, payable in installments if necessary, and to devote most of the additional income to staffing "service centers"

Increased voter participation in Chicano communities was CSO's highest priority and greatest achievement. After a decade of registration efforts, the organization claimed 450,000 new voters.

in each chapter office. Cesar Chavez, a leader turned organizer, had developed the service center concept in Oxnard. Opening the doors 18 hours a day and offering assistance on welfare, immigration, Social Security, and other common problems, he had attracted hundreds of walk-in clients, many of whom joined CSO.

After much debate the CSO leadership approved the dues increase, and several chapters created bustling service centers. But middle-class chapters saw the venture as expensive and irrelevant to their needs and gave it lukewarm support at best.

Class tensions came to a head at the 1962 CSO membership convention. Chavez, then director of organization, asked approval to expand a farm workers organizing project he had begun in Oxnard, where marches and sit-ins had forced growers to replace Mexican migrants with local Chicano workers. The convention turned him down. Chavez resigned to found the United Farm Workers of America, now affiliated with the AFL-CIO.

Some 17 CSO chapters have remained alive through the intervening decades, coordinated by Tony Rios, one of the founding members. But the surviving groups are pale shadows of their former selves, operating more as service agencies than as advocates for their communities. They bear witness to Chavez' pointed judgment: "The success of CSO tends to destroy it."

14

Only about ⅓ of the potential voting strength of the Spanish-speaking people is registered to vote in California.

REGISTER TO VOTE NOW!!

100% voting strength will give the Spanish-speaking population Justice and Equality.

415,600 Spanish-speaking U.S. citizens are NOT registered to vote in California

!!! JOIN CSO's MARCH !!!

Join CSO's 1960 Statewide Voter Registration Drive

15

ELECTORATE

CSO

CSO leaders and organizers, 1954. In the first row are City Councilman Eudardo Roybal (third from left), Fred Ross (fourth from left), and Cesar Chavez (far right). In the second row (far left) is Saul Alinsky.

16

Success also nurtured a destructive tendency in Back of the Yards. The Neighborhood Council, which by the early 1950's included 180 organizations, undertook an ambitious campaign to arrest housing deterioration and the flight of residents to the suburbs. With the support of local financial institutions, the Council helped thousands of individuals obtain loans to rehabilitate homes and storefronts. But while the campaign reversed the physical decline of the community, Alinsky came to distrust the motives of neighborhood leaders.

"Today," he wrote, "they are part of the city's establishment and are desperately trying to keep their community unchanged. They rationalize thus: they are not trying to keep blacks out but rather are trying to keep their people in. They are segregationists." He broke his ties with the Council and, in 1960, launched his first organizing project in a black community, the Woodlawn neighborhood south of the University of Chicago campus.

Once a fashionable residential district, Woodlawn had declined during the Depression when apartments were subdivided into cheaper units. After World War II it became a port of entry for thousands of migrants from the Deep South. By 1960, 89 percent of its population was black. Nearly a fourth of the residents were receiving some form of welfare and, though much of the housing was substandard, rents were higher than the city average.

The IAF was invited to Woodlawn by an ecumenical pastors alliance, which joined with a block club council and a businessmen's association to form the initial base of The Woodlawn Organization (TWO). Alinsky raised funds for the project from both the Catholic archdiocese and the United Presbyterian church. To some observers, the cooperation between Catholic and Protestant denominations was as momentous as the rapprochement in Back of the Yards between the Church and the CIO.

Alinsky preached that a young organization is like a prizefighter on the road to a championship: "You have to very carefully and selectively pick his opponents, knowing full well that certain defeats would be demoralizing and end his career." The idea is to start with issues offering a high probability of success, issues which are "immediate, specific, and realizable." TWO began by challenging local merchants who sold shoddy merchandise, overcharged, and enticed customers into installment purchases at usurious interest rates.

On March 6, 1961, one thousand people marched through the Woodlawn business district to kick off a "Square Deal" campaign. The following Saturday, TWO installed a scale and an adding machine in a neighborhood church so that customers who suspected underweighing or overcharging could verify their complaints. A community arbitration board with business and consumer representatives prodded merchants to conform with a "Code of Business Ethics." Leaflets urged residents to boycott offending stores. The campaign succeeded, according to Woodlawn leader Arthur Brazier: "Dishonest business practices sharply declined, TWO's prestige soared, and new groups joined the organization."

Turning its attention to housing issues, TWO honed the conflict tactics which were the hallmark of Alinsky's organizing theory. Following his principles—"pick the target, freeze it, personalize it, and polarize it"—the or-

**A billboard erected in Back of the Yards to publicize the Council's neighborhood conservation campaign.**

17

**A community congress in Woodlawn.** 18

ganization identified the most vulnerable landlords and demanded immediate repairs and better maintenance. Those who refused faced rent strikes and weekend picket lines at their homes. The appearance of black picketers wielding "Your Neighbor is a Slumlord" signs in white suburban neighborhoods was often sufficient to force the target and other recalcitrant landlords to the bargaining table.

TWO's formative years coincided with the rise of black protest in the South, and the Southern movement exercised a strong influence on the organization. Inspired by a meeting with CORE Freedom Riders, Woodlawn leaders even staged a "Northern freedom ride" in August, 1961, when a cavalcade of 40 buses brought 2000 neighborhood residents to City Hall to register to vote. But the object of the action was not civil rights; it was to show Mayor Richard Daley that TWO, like the fabled Chicago machine, could deliver voters. Although race shaped the dynamic of TWO, the organization engaged racial issues on a different plane than the freedom movement, seeking power and "self-determination" for one black community.

Self-determination was at the core of TWO's protracted battle against an urban renewal plan sponsored by the University of Chicago and the City. The initial proposal, released in 1960, promised Woodlawn more "removal" than renewal; it called for the university to annex a mile-long strip of the neighborhood. Subsequent revi-

"City Hall used to be a forbidden place, but we've made so many trips there and seen so many people that it's beginning to feel like a neighborhood store."

a TWO leader

sions offered little more, since planners hardly bothered to ascertain the wishes of neighborhood residents. When the City Planning Department issued its final recommendations in March 1962, a department spokesman explained the absence of community input: "There is nobody to speak for the community," he insisted. "A community does not exist in Woodlawn."

One week after the City's announcement, 1200 delegates representing 97 groups at TWO's community congress issued this response: "We will not be planned for as though we were children." The organization hired its own planners to critique the City proposal and devise an alternative. Neighborhood leaders did not expect to halt university expansion, but they hoped to use their opposition as leverage to obtain more low-income housing for the community.

THIS MIGHTY DREAM   111

TWO's 1962 campaign to desegregate public schools focused on neighborhood issues of overcrowded and inferior facilities. Above, Woodlawn parents brave sub-zero temperatures to protest the use of an abandoned building as a school, attempting to block a School Board truck from reaching the premises.

A sit-in at Mayor Daley's office by 600 Woodlawn residents forced Daley to negotiate; he agreed to give TWO a majority of seats on the project supervisory committee and a veto over the selection of the project manager. He also promised that no demolition would occur until new housing was built for displaced residents. The City eventually allocated urban renewal funds for a 502-unit low-income housing project, known as "Woodlawn Gardens," which was planned, constructed, owned, and managed by TWO.

After the "War on Poverty" opened in the mid-1960s, TWO obtained federal grants to establish experimental, community-controlled programs in education and youth employment. But City Hall would not tolerate the competition, and the machine used its political muscle to shut off the federal spigot. TWO then shifted to projects, such as a supermarket, day care centers, and further housing development, which were less threatening to City Hall and less reliant on government funding. The organization shunned controversy and sought conciliatory relationships with former adversaries; the explicitly political goal of "self-determination" evolved into the more ambiguous "self-help." At its tenth anniversary, TWO adopted a new slogan—"From Protest to Program."

TWO's self-help doctrine typified one strategy adopted by black activists grappling with the problems of the urban poor. Their aim was to develop an economic base in low-income communities independent of both government and the corporate economy. Other veterans of the civil rights movement took a sharply divergent course, emphasizing immediate gains in income over the long-term prospects of economic development, and assigning government the primary role in eradicating poverty. They founded a militant movement of welfare recipients, the poorest of the poor, and adopted the blunt slogan, "More Money Now."

"From Protest to Program": TWO members sort groceries from a community supermarket owned and managed by the organization.

## Welfare Rights

The paradox of "poverty amidst plenty" surfaced on the national political agenda during the early 1960s. Much of its impetus derived from the civil rights movement. Although less than one-quarter of the country's poor were non-white, more than half of the minority population lived below the official poverty line. As black unrest moved north to the urban ghettos and shifted to economic grievances, national political leaders were compelled to respond. In his first state of the union address in January 1964, President Johnson declared an "unconditional war on poverty."

Congress swiftly enacted an array of programs to enhance public services in low-income communities. The legislation mandated "maximum feasible participation" by community residents in the planning and delivery of new services such as day care, legal aid, and pre-school education. Rather than diminishing protest, however, the War on Poverty spawned ghetto organizations which denounced the programs as band-aid solutions. Critics inside and outside the ghettos insisted that the answer to poverty was not more services for the poor but more income.

Income for many poor Americans meant the welfare system, a federal-state hodgepodge descended from New Deal-era relief programs. The most striking feature of the system was its patchy coverage. In 1964, only 8.8 million of the nation's 34 million impoverished households were receiving public assistance; the majority were single mothers and their dependent children, whose average annual benefit—$1752 for a family of four—left them far below the poverty level of $3240. A combination of restrictive state rules, degrading intake procedures, and the stigma associated with welfare had discouraged many eligible persons from applying.

But the quantity of applicants began to rise in the mid-1960s. Anti-poverty agencies informed the poor of their legal right to welfare and how to assert it, while War on Poverty rhetoric erased some of the stigma. "Welfare rights" groups sprang up in New York, Los Angeles, Boston, Cleveland, and other cities to challenge eligibility restrictions and low benefits. Some were organized by recipients, some by poverty program workers—often former civil rights activists—and some by community organizers in the Alinsky tradition, trained by Fred Ross in Syracuse, New York.

In 1965, activist professors Richard Cloward and Frances Fox Piven advanced a plan to transform these isolated groups into a national movement. Their "strategy to end poverty" rested on the premise that for every person collecting welfare at least one other eligible individual was not receiving benefits. Mobilizing this vast pool to apply for assistance would provoke a fiscal and political crisis, they reasoned, and just as the Birmingham and Selma crises had produced civil rights legislation, a welfare crisis would compel the governing Democrats to introduce a comprehensive income program.

George Wiley, associate national director of CORE, was among the first to respond to Piven and Cloward's proposal. Like many civil rights veterans he was seeking new ways to mobilize the urban poor. After CORE adopted a racially separatist course, Wiley resigned his post and established the Poverty/Rights Action Center to develop a community organizing strategy with welfare as its initial focus.

An Ohio coalition of welfare recipients and church-based supporters lit a spark in the spring of 1966 with its plan for a 150-mile "Walk for Adequate Welfare." Wiley seized the opportunity, encouraging other local groups to stage simultaneous demonstrations on June 30. Well over 6000 protestors turned out in 25 cities. To the media Wiley trumpeted the event as "the birth of a movement."

On the heels of this success, recipient leaders and organizers from 11 states met in Chicago and laid the

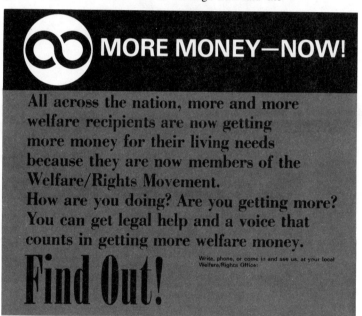

groundwork for the National Welfare Rights Organization (NWRO). Johnnie Tillmon, who would become the organization's first national chairman, describes the tenor of the meeting:

"It was a very different experience. In the past, most of us had been so ashamed that we were on welfare that we wouldn't even admit it to another welfare recipient. But as we talked to each other, we forgot about that shame, and as we listened to the terrible treatment and conditions all over the country, we could begin thinking about the idea that maybe it wasn't us that should be ashamed."

The delegates adopted a statement of purpose which articulated two fundamental principles. It asserted that society must guarantee every individual an adequate income, either through employment or public assistance.

22

23

"Basic needs" campaigns were the mainstay of welfare rights organizing. Above, Washington, DC recipients camp out in a downtown park in the course of a battle for furniture allowances. Below, welfare mothers demanding winter clothing for their children are arrested in front of the Washtenaw County Building in Ann Arbor, MI, September 1968.

And consistent with the notion of welfare as a right, it demanded dignity for recipients—elimination of all the petty harassments and degradations endemic to the system.

Questions of strategy and structure were deferred to a national coordinating committee. Wiley, who assumed the role of national director, had already resolved certain elements. While he accepted the crisis-producing strategy espoused by Piven and Cloward, he intended to avoid those aspects he viewed as manipulative. Instead of mass mobilizations which left little organization behind, he envisioned a permanent, community-based membership organization. Rather than creating a crisis and "praying for the best," Wiley hoped to capture sufficient political power to control the outcome.

NWRO ultimately adopted a formal structure which was "carefully designed," according to staffer Ed Day, "to ensure that we would truly have an indigenous group of poor people. We didn't want these groups taken over by church people or social work people or other do-gooders." By-laws restricted chapter membership to persons with incomes below the poverty line; affluent supporters, organized as "Friends of Welfare Rights," did not have voting privileges at the biannual conventions which selected national leaders.

The organization sought to maintain indigenous control by establishing a clear distinction between elected leadership and paid staff, following Alinsky's precepts in this regard rather than the looser style of the civil rights movement. Recipient leaders were the final arbiters on organizational policy and, excepting Wiley, the most visible public figures in the movement.

By the end of 1966, NWRO had grown to 170 active affiliates in 60 cities. The initial burst of organizing activity diverged from the Piven-Cloward script by focusing on existing recipients, a pattern that would shape the movement. The most successful campaigns targeted "basic needs" allowances—supplemental grants for furniture, appliances, and clothing which were authorized by law but rarely provided.

New York City groups pioneered the "basic needs" strategy in 1965 when they stormed welfare offices to demand emergency clothing allowances; several days of protest produced checks of $50-$100 for hundreds of families. Recognizing the recruitment value of campaigns that delivered immediate benefits to protestors, the NWRO national office cranked out a "how-to" kit labeled "More Money Now" which contained a list of all items due recipients under law and mimeographed application forms. Organizers distributed thousands of the kits with flyers announcing local meetings. The meetings became staging sessions for protests; after completing the special allowance applications, recipients would march on the welfare centers to submit the forms *en masse* and demand immediate action.

NWRO launched nationally coordinated "basic needs" campaigns: school clothing in late summer, winter clothing in the fall, Easter clothing in early spring, furniture campaigns in between. In Massachusetts, chief organizer Bill Pastreich introduced a new dimension to the strategy, requiring recipients to join the organization and pay dues before receiving kits or any other form of assistance. Pastreich's squad of young organizers built new groups in virtually assembly-line fashion, recruiting door-to-door intensively for six to eight weeks prior to each founding meeting. This method, which became known as the "Boston Model," was widely imitated by other NWRO affiliates.

Victories generated momentum; demands and tactics escalated. After a Massachusetts sit-in secured on-the-spot grants of $600-$1000 for household furnishings, Boston WRO leader Roberta O'Neil vowed, "We're not leaving until we get telephones." The state welfare commissioner was summoned and, more than nine hours after the sit-in began, he acquiesced to that demand as well. Sit-ins sometimes became sleep-ins, lasting several days; angry demonstrators ransacked welfare offices; at least once, in Springfield, Massachusetts, a riot ensued. But the campaigns almost always delivered the goods. In New York City, for example, more than $10 million a month was being disbursed for "basic needs" by the summer of 1968.

As welfare costs mounted, several states established "flat grant" systems which eliminated separate allowances for clothing and household goods. By abolishing the prime source of membership benefits, the flat grant stymied welfare rights organizing wherever it was introduced. Other factors aggravated the difficulty of sustaining growth. Welfare departments established formal grievance procedures which undercut the need for group action. NWRO's elaborate structure sheltered leaders who viewed new membership drives as a threat to their status. Some critics claimed that the Boston Model stunted long-term development by emphasizing quick results and by relying too heavily on professional organizers.

Membership in the flagship NWRO chapters of New York and Massachusetts declined precipitously after 1968, when flat grants were introduced in those states. Elsewhere the movement continued to grow. To assist expansion, NWRO devised new nationally coordinated campaigns on poverty-related issues such as free school lunch programs and utility deposit requirements. A successful campaign in Philadelphia to secure credit for welfare recipients at a local department store inspired a national boycott of Sears outlets in 1969. Picket lines and "shop-in" actions did not budge Sears, but Montgomery Ward, fearing similar disruptions, agreed to extend up to $100 credit to 2000 NWRO members in selected locations.

New chapters sprouted in smaller cities and rural areas, often quite spontaneously. In Waltham, Massachusetts, for example, Terry Szpak, left homeless with three children, was infuriated when told it would take 30

## 24

NWRO issued an array of buttons, flags, stickers, and other paraphrenalia emblazoned with audacious slogans. For a stigmatized class, these visual emblems of solidarity expressed a new-found self-esteem and emerging sense of power.

George Wiley and welfare rights leaders. NWRO officers, all recipients, mirrored the organization's overwhelmingly female and black membership.

26 **Zap FAP! The fight against President Nixon's Family Assistance Plan combined shrewd appeals to liberal sentiments and militant direct action. Above, members occupy the DC welfare department building after breaking down the doors. Center, NWRO vice-chair Beulah Sanders negotiates with an agency official during an all-day sit-in at HEW Secretary Robert Finch's office. Right, NWRO asked sympathizers to live on a welfare budget for a week.**

days to process her welfare application. "I had read about Mothers for Adequate Welfare in the paper," she recalls. "I wrote to them and asked how I could start one of their groups. . . we asked for the use of a church and a hundred people showed up. I had expected two or three. I didn't know what to do but somehow we managed to start a group."

By 1969, NWRO claimed 30,000 members in 100 cities; the organization celebrated its third birthday with simultaneous demonstrations in 19 state capitals and places as remote as North Dakota's Turtle Mountain Reservation. New groups in the Southwest and Appalachian regions brought more white and Hispanic members, stirring Wiley's dream of a multi-racial movement. But in the northern cities membership remained almost exclusively black and female, and it was the more aggressive big-city protests which captured the headlines. NWRO was typecast in the public mind as an organization of militant black women, an image which sharpened the emerging backlash against welfare costs and welfare activism.

For there was now a genuine welfare crisis. Between December 1964 and February 1969, the Aid to Families

with Dependent Children (AFDC) caseload rose by more than 1.5 million families, a staggering 71 percent increase. Although NWRO had abandoned the strategy of mobilizing new applicants, disruptive welfare rights demonstrations coupled with ghetto unrest had prompted welfare adminstrators to loosen restrictions. Lawsuits filed on behalf of NWRO had generated a series of Supreme Court rulings which liberalized eligibility standards and erected procedural safeguards against arbitrary terminations of benefits.

The spiralling cost of welfare forced governors and local officials to seek fiscal relief from Washington. They found an ally in newly elected President Richard Nixon. In August 1969, Nixon proposed a Family Assistance Plan (FAP) to replace the welfare patchwork with a federally guaranteed annual income of $1600 for a family of four.

NWRO jumped immediately into the legislative fray. Although the organization had mounted some Washington actions, including an unprecedented sit-in at Senate Finance Committee hearings, national policy advocacy had previously been subordinated to grassroots organizing. But when FAP was introduced, NWRO's membership base was eroding and local chapters were encountering increased resistance to their demands. Compared with the dismal prospects for local victories, national welfare reform looked promising.

The Nixon Administration had carefully tailored FAP to appeal to a broad range of the political spectrum. Governors welcomed it wholeheartedly. Welfare rights supporters applauded its "entitlement" aspect, feeling

# Live like a dog Dec. 1-7.

### Test President Nixon's welfare plan.

19¢: Breakfast
19¢: Lunch
19¢: Dinner

For more information contact your local Council of Churches or your local Welfare Rights Organization.

**National Welfare Rights Organization.**

28

that a guaranteed income program would entail less stigma and bureaucratic tyranny than traditional forms of public assistance. Conservatives noted that FAP promised to halt the growth of the welfare rolls by forcing recipients to accept jobs at less than minimum wage, and that the $1600 income standard was lower than existing AFDC benefit levels in all but six Southern states.

Initially NWRO endorsed the concept while demanding a much higher minimum standard. But as congressional conservatives moved to make the program more restrictive, the organization shifted to a new position: "Zap FAP." Mass protests at the Washington, D.C. Welfare Department and a sit-in at the office of U.S. Health, Education, and Welfare Secretary Robert Finch polarized the issue. In November 1970, an unusual coalition of fiscal conservatives and a few liberals swayed by NWRO's opposition defeated the Nixon bill.

With national welfare reform on ice, states began instituting their own "reforms." In January 1971, Nevada struck 21 percent of its AFDC recipients from the rolls and reduced payments to another 28 percent. NWRO launched "Operation Nevada" to reverse the cuts, organizing mass marches on Las Vegas casinos while a "lawyer's brigade" pursued legal remedies. A court ruling in March reinstated all recipients and ordered retroactive benefits. Although Operation Nevada proved successful, it was NWRO's last major local campaign.

The fight for a guaranteed income continued at the national level with a "Children's March" in Washington D.C. and action on the Democratic Party. In coalition with SCLC and the National Tenants Organization,

NWRO presented a Poor People's Platform at the 1972 Democratic Convention; the guaranteed income plank received 1000 delegate votes in a televised roll call. But these campaigns were quixotic attempts to beat back the tide. Nixon and other politicians roused voters in the 1972 campaign with vicious attacks on "welfare cheaters," while George McGovern's advocacy of a $4000 guaranteed income crippled his presidential bid. FAP had been defeated a second time and welfare reform disappeared from the national agenda. With the ebbing of black protest, politicians no longer felt compelled to acknowledge the isolated and scapegoated minority which NWRO represented.

Wiley argued for broadening the organizational base

"Operation Nevada" in the winter of 1971 forced state welfare officials to restore public assistance benefits, but NWRO was unable to prevent 19 other states from implementing welfare cuts that year.

by adding other low-income constituencies. But the neglect of local organizing in favor of national lobbying after 1969 had taken a severe toll on NWRO, and it was too ridden with internal conflict to attempt a bold change in direction. Wiley left to found the Movement for Economic Justice, an effort to test his concept of a broad-based poor people's movement. His sudden death in 1973 deprived the experiment of a nationally recognized leader. NWRO declared bankruptcy the following year, although chapters survive in scattered locales.

While it did not achieve its primary objectives—a permanent organization of the poor and a guaranteed adequate income—the welfare rights movement had a substantial impact on both the perception and the reality of poverty in the United States. It politicized the central question of income distribution. It strengthened the belief that all persons have a right to basic subsistence, and it identified the state as the guarantor of that principle. It taught the poorest of the poor not to be embarrassed to assert their rights. And it delivered billions of dollars of public assistance to millions of poor people.

To the tradition of social protest in the United States, NWRO left two legacies. One was the example, defying conventional wisdom, of a powerful organization led by poor black women. The other was a generation of professional organizers who would infuse NWRO's militant spirit and deliberate techniques into the mainstream of community organizing.

## ACORN

By 1970 the strategic impasse of the welfare rights movement was plainly evident. Other movements which had issued from minority ghettos and college campuses in the previous decade were similarly isolated and floundering. Activists continued to press radical demands for social change, but they foundered on the increasingly vocal and intransigent opposition of working-class whites, who felt that their own grievances had been brushed aside in the headlong attack on poverty and racial discrimination.

Organizers concluded that social change movements would remain isolated and vulnerable until they developed broader, multi-racial constituencies spanning the social chasm between homeowner and public housing tenant, between skilled blue-collar worker and welfare recipient—between moderate- and low-income Americans. This quest for a "majority constituency" became the central motif of community protest in the 1970s, a motif vividly expressed in the evolution of ACORN, the largest contemporary community organization.

ACORN was a child of the welfare rights movement crossed with the Alinsky organizing tradition, and like most offspring it both resembled its parents and sought to avoid their errors. When George Wiley sent NWRO organizer Wade Rathke to Little Rock, Arkansas, in June 1970, they shared a tacit understanding that Rathke intended to build a new type of poor people's organization on a welfare rights foundation. Rathke envisioned a statewide, neighborhood-based operation, genuinely multi-racial, which would address the entire range of problems affecting low- and moderate-income Arkansans.

With a Southern heritage of racial separation, a conservative political environment, and a negligible history of community protest, Arkansas offered an acid test for this experiment. It also furnished a protective incubator, far from the centers of national power and the intrusive glare of the national media.

The first organizing effort upon Rathke's arrival in Little Rock was a standard "basic needs" campaign. Citing an obscure regulation, hundreds of recipients stormed the state welfare office to demand free furniture. The militant action took the state by surprise and embarrassed Governor Winthrop Rockefeller, who owed his office to liberal and black voters. With a reelection bid pending, Rockefeller established a new agency which distributed used furniture, appliances, and clothing to more than 1000 families.

In the midst of the "furniture for families" battle, Rathke introduced the name ACORN—Arkansas Community Organizations for Reform Now. The new organization soon took form as an alignment of "working poor" and "welfare poor" with campaigns for free lunches in the schools, tenant rights in public housing, and improved

Panic selling, fostered by realtors playing on fears of racial transition, infected central Little Rock neighborhoods in the early 1970s. ACORN groups mobilized black and white residents to fight blockbusting and posted signs like these to signal a shared commitment to the neighborhood.

emergency care at hospitals. ACORN diverged further from the welfare rights norm in the summer of 1971 when it organized groups of Vietnam veterans and unemployed workers, acquiring a substantial male membership for the first time.

These changes were welcomed by some Arkansas welfare rights leaders, such as Gloria Wilson. "The welfare reform issue was dying out," she recalls. "It didn't have enough in it for most people. There were too many other issues, like tax reform, which Welfare Rights just didn't take in." Other leaders complained that dilution of the welfare rights emphasis was turning ACORN into a "middle-class lobbying group." The result was a bitter split; ACORN disaffiliated with NWRO, and several prominent welfare leaders severed ties with ACORN.

The conflict left a sour aftertaste, but it freed ACORN to crack a moderate-income, homeowning constituency. Between June and December 1972, organizers built eight community groups in the older, declining neighborhoods of central Little Rock and more than doubled ACORN's active membership. Under the slogan "Save the City," the new groups demanded parks, drainage, and street improvements and attacked threats to their neighborhoods from commercial encroachment, freeway construction, and racial blockbusting. ACORN signs proclaiming "We Like It Here—This House is *Not* For Sale" sprouted on dozens of lawns in the central city.

The vehicle for the Save the City drive was a systematic and detailed organizing model—descended from Fred Ross' methods and the WRO "Boston model"—which enabled a young, inexperienced field staff to create functioning neighborhood groups in six to eight weeks. ACORN consciously sacrificed institutional depth for autonomy and rapid growth. In place of

the painstaking courtship of community institutions decreed by Alinsky, a process which could absorb a year or more, the model prescribed intensive door-to-door recruitment. Doorknocking casts a wide net, snaring unaffiliated residents like Bill Whipple, a fiercely independent small businessman.

"I'd never been a joiner of groups," Whipple says. "But one day, why some young lady came by and wanted to talk to me for a few minutes. . .I gave her a dollar and since I had a dollar invested I went to the first meeting of the neighborhood group. . .If they'd asked me to join by mail, I'd probably have thrown it away."

Against his own wishes, Whipple's neighborhood group elected him an officer at its first meeting, and within months he was leading protests at City Hall. While IAF-style organizations drew upon experienced activists from their church, labor, and social affiliates, ACORN's wide-open structure often thrust novices into front-line roles. The leaders who emerged sometimes lacked polish, but they were unfettered by competing organizational and political loyalties.

Without an institutional network to sustain it, ACORN stressed individual membership dues. Self-sufficiency, based on dues, would not only assure the independence of the organization but would establish a direct measure of accountability. "ACORN lives or dies based on its membership's willingness to organize and pay their dues," Rathke argues. "It doesn't matter if I or the governor or anyone else thinks we're doing great. If the membership stops paying dues we're out of business."

Consumers advocating utility rate structure reforms became a fixture at state Public Service Commission hearings.

## 31

32

33

The reluctance of regulatory authorities to institute sweeping reforms in the rate structure compelled ACORN to take the issue to the voters. A Lifeline initiative carried Little Rock in 1976 only to be voided by state courts. Above, members collect petition signatures to place the initiative on the ballot.

Replicated in hundreds of neighborhoods over a decade of growth, the ACORN-model organizing drive produced a dues-paying membership of more than 50,000 in 25 states. The initial expansion occurred in Arkansas, where ACORN opened six regional offices in 1973-74. This was the era of the first "energy crisis," when the utility companies scrambled to build and finance new power plants, and soaring utility bills provoked outrage from poor and affluent alike. After years of political immunity, the regulated utilities were suddenly vulnerable, and ACORN took advantage of their weakness.

In September 1973, the Arkansas Power and Light Company (AP&L) announced plans to build a giant coal-fired generating plant in the soybean and cotton country southeast of Little Rock. After determining that the plant's chemical emissions could harm agriculture, ACORN organized growers in the vicinity of the plant site. The irate farmers forced the issue onto the front pages with a series of flashy maneuvers: demanding a $50 million "damage deposit" from the company, disrupting an airborne promotional tour for press and state officials, asking Harvard University—the largest stockholder in AP&L's parent company—to conduct an independent environmental impact study. The state Public Service Commission ultimately cut the plant's size in half.

When AP&L and other utility companies requested rate hikes from the Public Service Commission, hundreds of ACORN members conducted protest vigils at company offices and stormed commission hearings to deliver testimony against the increases. They condemned the common practice of awarding volume discount rates to large industrial and commercial users and demanded a special low rate, known as "Lifeline," for basic residential needs. Responding to the first major rate protest in May 1974, the Commission slashed a rate hike request by $6 million and credited ACORN with influencing its decision. A year later, the Commission ordered the Arkansas-

Louisiana Gas Company to institute a more equitable rate structure.

The utility rate campaigns exemplified the tactics of community protest in the 1970s. Though occasionally raucous, the actions were not disruptive enough to disturb the regular functioning of business and government, nor were they large enough, in themselves, to impress elected officials. But the protests transformed a dry, technical issue into a dramatic confrontation between "the people" and "the interests," and the media broadcast this confrontation to thousands of disgruntled utility consumers. Many came to support ACORN's position. Politicians recognized the appeal of rate reform and built successful campaigns on the issue.

Involving every social element in Arkansas from soybean farmers and small businessmen to suburban homeowners, the utility protests cemented ACORN's image as a broad-based, statewide organization. Whereas

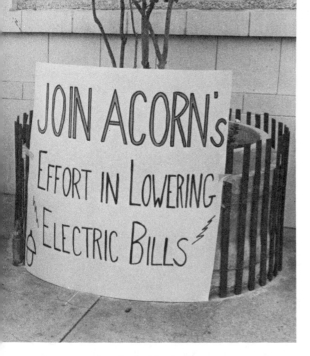

Gloria Wilson

Bill Whipple

Steve McDonald

Elena Hanggi

Elizabeth Martinez

Grover Wright

35

previous campaigns had addressed local concerns such as zoning, roads, and recreation, the demand for rate reform was perceived as a challenge to the state's dominant economic interests. "The utility companies are the most powerful corporations in Arkansas," notes Walter Nunn, a Little Rock political scientist. "By taking them on, ACORN entered the big leagues."

ACORN's successes were not unique. In Chicago, the Citizens Action Program had blocked an inner-city expressway and was generating pressure against banks to increase mortgage lending in low- and moderate-income neighborhoods. Massachusetts Fair Share had organized thousands of homeowners to protest inequities in auto insurance rates and property tax assessments, while the Citizens Action League in California had lobbied a Lifeline measure through the state legislature. Despite differences in organizing style and technique, all of these efforts were grounded in the "majority constituency" idea. As such groups expanded and multiplied across the

**Property tax inequities, like utility rates, proved to be a fertile issue for community organizations seeking a moderate income constituency. Below, an ACORN delegation exposes untaxed bank assets and urges a county assessor to add them to the property tax rolls.**

34

## "MAJORITY CONSTITUENCY"

Like the Southern Tenant Farmers Union, ACORN was founded in Arkansas with a rigorous commitment to build a multi-racial organization. A concern with sexual equality emerged later.

"**When I first started, there was a strong male hierarchy,**" recalls Elena Hanggi. "**It manifested itself at board meetings, for instance. They'd say, 'This is what we've decided, and what you say is all well and good, but this is what we've decided.' But that has changed dramatically. I think our members are getting much better about looking at your qualifications— not whether you're male, female, black or white.**"

Hanggi was elected president of the Association Board in 1983.

## 37

36

Neighborhood campaigns: Left, Jefferson Park Area Community Organization in Denver protests traffic congestion and spillover parking from nearby Mile High Stadium. Right, members of Jeffries Boulevard Action Group take their complaints about trash in vacant lots to a Detroit city official.

country, organizers waxed optimistic, convinced that they had found the strategic key to social change.

Between 1975 and 1980, ACORN spread beyond Arkansas to more than 40 communities, penetrating big city ghettos and Sun Belt trailer parks, Texas barrios and Midwestern subdivisions. ACORN groups fought urban renewal schemes in Detroit, toxic chemical threats in Memphis, tenant evictions in Reno. A new organizational entity known as the "Association" took shape, governed by a board composed of two elected delegates from each affiliated state.

Growth exposed a latent tension within the leadership between a commitment to local issues and organization and a more expansive conception of ACORN's role. Expansion per se was not at issue. In contrast to Alinsky, who was suspicious of large organizations and espoused

**Spring 1978: The flyers said, "Need a job? Call ACORN." Hundreds of teenagers did; they stormed employment offices in half a dozen cities with applications for summer work. The jobs campaign marked a resurgence of disruptive action after a period of more restrained tactics.**

38

strict neighborhood autonomy, Rathke had deliberately fostered a common membership identity which transcended local loyalties and implicitly identified growth with organizational health. But some leaders questioned the pace of expansion, fearing that it would divert resources from existing operations and entangle ACORN in divisive national issues. Others, including Association Board president Steve McDonald, countered that neighborhood problems were inseparable from the policies made in Washington, D.C. Neither could be tackled without an organization wielding national power.

A soft-spoken Vietnam veteran, disabled by multiple sclerosis, McDonald was widely respected for his self-effacing direction of the board. His firm insistence on the primacy of "organizing the unorganized," backed by a consensus among senior staff members, carried the expansion issue on several decisive occasions.

The outcome of the debate established that ACORN's fundamental commitment was not to specific neighborhoods, or even to neighborhood organizing, but to its low- and moderate-income constituency. This ambitious commitment pushed ACORN well beyond the historic boundaries of community protest. In late 1977, the Association board authorized an experimental effort to organize low-wage and unemployed workers; it evolved into full-fledged union drives among hotel, restaurant, and home care workers. The same year saw the formation of a "media project" which generated radio stations in Tampa, Dallas, and Little Rock. But ACORN's most significant departure from conventional practice was its encounter with national party politics in the presidential campaign year 1980.

While community organizations had generally shunned electoral activity as diversionary and divisive, ACORN had never observed this taboo. "Victories are won on the streets," Rathke contends, "but they are ratified at the polls." The organization had endorsed candidates for local office as early as 1972, and in one

> "Most of us joined ACORN because we were concerned with conditions in our neighborhoods. But we came to realize that we couldn't win what we wanted for our communities if we didn't get involved in bigger issues.
>
> In order to win the things we want, we have to grow in every way. More power in our cities means that we have to organize more neighborhoods. More power for poor and working people means we need to be in more cities, in more states.
>
> The growth and development that is essential to our goals can put a lot of strain on our organization. But we can't afford to protect what we have won so far at the expense of what we can and must win in the future."
>
> Mary Ellen Smith
> Philadelphia ACORN

# Do You Care About Your NEIGHBORHOOD?
## THESE MEN DO

**Perlesta A. Hollingsworth**, Position 6, City Director

*Perlesta A. Hollingsworth: "The wishes of the people should carry more way than the businesses in determining land use of the city. Our neighborhoods must be preserved."*

**Jack Young**, Position 7, City Director

*Jack Young: "People from the East and South ends of the city have not been represented or heard by the city Board. I intend to help the people—black or white—from those areas to get involved in city government."*

## VOTE
## FOR YOUR NEIGHBORHOOD
ENDORSED BY:
**APAC—ACORN Political Action Committee**
523 W. 15th Street   Little Rock, Arkansas 72202   376-7151

39

**Breaking with the anti-electoral tradition in community organizing, ACORN chapters frequently backed candidates for public office.**

40

**"ACORN 80": Above, members rally outside the Democratic mid-term convention in Memphis, TN, December 1978. Below, Wilma Lee questions presidential candidate Edward Kennedy about his stand on the "People's Platform," Davenport, IA, December 1979.**

41

memorable instance had elected 190 Arkansas members and allies to the Pulaski County Quorum Court, constituting a near majority of that archaic legislature.

"ACORN 80" was contrived to exploit the distinctive features of the presidential nominating process—its exhaustive itinerary, its local/national interplay, its saturation media coverage, its central place in contemporary political mythology. Leaders hoped that a combination of direct action protest and strategic intervention in the nominating process would force the national parties to pay more attention to the concerns of low- and moderate-income Americans.

The opening salvo was fired in Memphis on December 9, 1978, when more than 1000 demonstrators marched and chanted outside the Democratic Party's mid-term convention. Over the next six months, ACORN members laboriously fashioned a consensus national platform. Derived mainly from local campaign experience, this "People's Platform" identified nine priority concerns—mostly bread-and-butter issues like housing, energy, and health care—and advanced detailed policy planks in each area. The planks ran the gamut from minor tinkering to radical restructuring of government and the economy.

While some local political activists embraced the People's Platform, leaders of both major parties politely dismissed it. ACORN members were especially angered by the Democrats, self-proclaimed "Party of the People." They attributed the Party's reluctance to acknowledge the depth of their grievances to the meager representation of low- and moderate-income Democrats at national con-

ventions and other policy-making conclaves. ACORN demanded a national Party commission to redress under-representation and ensure the Party's accountability to its historic base.

During the 1980 primary season, ACORN members invaded precinct and district caucuses to press resolutions backing the commission demand and to elect convention delegates pledged to support it. The organization declined to endorse incumbent Jimmy Carter or his challenger, Senator Edward Kennedy, allowing affiliates to choose on the basis of local membership sentiment and political expediency. In Carter strongholds like Florida and South Dakota, ACORN members won slots as Carter delegates to the Democratic National Convention; in Missouri, they ran uncommitted; in Michigan, a massive ACORN turn-out at inner-city district caucuses provided winning margins for Kennedy.

ACORN played by the Party rules, but it also broke them on occasion. Members sat in at Carter headquarters in Philadelphia and massed outside Democratic National Committee offices in Washington, D.C., to demand a meeting with John White, the elusive Party chairman. Unaccustomed to such "inside-outside" tactics, the Democrats succumbed and authorized a 15-member Commission. Chaired by Congressman Mickey Leland of Texas, the commission developed an array of recommendations which might have increased the visibility and influence of low- and moderate-income Democrats in the presidential nominating process. But Party leaders rejected all but the most cosmetic proposals. Elizabeth Martinez, one of two ACORN representatives on the commission, denounced the final product as "just a few crumbs," and the organization was left with little to show for its efforts beyond an enhanced reputation for political action.

"ACORN 80" did fulfill important internal objectives, however. National actions and conventions, the platform development process, and the involvement of every state affiliate in coordinated action towards a common goal had transformed a multi-state association into a unified national organization. The campaign had defined a militant style and a radical program. Members who could not accept one or the other gradually dropped out of the ranks.

As the '80s opened, other community organizations were also pursuing national strategies. A network of groups, consolidating under the banner of "National People's Action," had obtained an unprecedented agreement from the Aetna Insurance Company to make policies available in deteriorated neighborhoods and to reinvest millions of dollars in inner-city housing rehabilitation. Massachusetts Fair Share had joined with other advocacy organizations and labor unions in a Citizen/Labor Energy Coalition which successfully challenged the deregulation of natural gas. Among the major networks in community organizing, only the Industrial Areas Foundation, carriers of the orthodox Alinsky mantle, resisted the impulse to "go national."

**A Philadelphia squatter claims a home.**

But the ACORN of the '80s had diverged from the other national networks; it was quite different, in fact, from the ACORN of the mid-'70s. While some organizations had drifted toward the "high end" of the majority constituency—moderate-income homeowners and union-wage workers—ACORN's membership was increasingly low-income and minority. While community protest tactics had generally remained demonstrative in character, ACORN's were increasingly disruptive. While many organizations were trying to stabilize their operations through coalitions with churches and unions, ACORN was gambling with risky mobilizations.

The squatters campaign of 1981-82 embodied all of these trends. Squatting began in Philadelphia, where an exceptional cadre of leaders and organizers had built an innovative, militant organization. Decrying the contradiction between the city's 30,000 abandoned houses and its shortage of low-income housing, Philadelphia ACORN asked the municipality to institute a large-scale homesteading program which would convey vacant houses to people in need. When the City failed to respond, the organization recruited hundreds of low-income families to seize, occupy, and repair abandoned structures.

"We had no choice," asserts Philadelphia chairman Grover Wright. "Some say squatting is illegal, but we say letting houses sit empty is immoral." The tactic spread to Detroit and St. Louis, thence to a dozen other cities. Squatters were evicted and arrested in St. Louis, Pittsburgh, and Dallas, but forced concessions from city officials in Philadelphia, Ft. Worth, Detroit, and Tulsa. In June 1982, 200 squatters journeyed to Washington, D.C. to erect a tent city behind the White House. They assailed the nationwide housing shortage and demanded reforms in the federal homesteading program. Congress responded, more than a year later, with legislation ex-

43

**Supporters stave off a squatter's eviction in Ft. Worth.**

panding the program and targeting it to a lower-income constituency.

For ACORN, the squatters campaign was the culmination of a five-year quest to recover the audacity and militance of its welfare rights origins—qualities which had been diluted in the pursuit of a majority constituency. More recently, ACORN has moved closer to the contemporary mainstream, organizing a national coalition of labor, church, minority, and peace groups to challenge the policies of President Ronald Reagan. Such periodic swings are characteristic of ACORN's evolutionary pattern: a continual dialectic between low- and moderate-income, mobilization and organization, expansion and consolidation, militance and accommodation.

Community organizing has been the most forceful expression of social protest since the eclipse of the civil rights movement. But though ACORN and its brethren have organized thousands of families, they have not yet approached the millions mobilized by agrarian, labor, and civil rights insurgencies. While they have won impressive individual victories on a local and national scale, they have not had a great collective impact on the configuration of power in the United States.

These shortcomings are partly attributable to historical circumstance. Community organizing matured during an era of political alienation and economic contraction, which impeded recruitment and made "targets" more resistant to protest. But the defects of the organizations themselves must also be acknowledged. Some have fallen prey to racism, parochialism, and cooptation. Even those that have maintained a generous vision of empowerment still seek a strategy to realize it. The missing element is a mass response. Whether community organizing can generate a movement dynamic to complement its sophisticated techniques will determine whether it matches its predecessors as an agent of social change.

44

**ACORN squatters established a tent city in Washington, DC, and presented exuberant testimony to a U.S. House sub-committee, June 1982.**

45

# Conclusion

Why do reasonable men and women risk their health and their jobs, their property and reputations—all the precarious assets of their lives—for a dream of justice? The conventional response, that they "have no choice," is hardly credible. Rebellion is rare even under the most oppressive conditions; there are always sound reasons to believe that action is futile, change impossible. Yet in defiance of all rational expectation, Americans have chosen at certain times to picket in freezing rain, march miles on scorched roads, stand fast before police dogs and firehoses.

Our wonder is not so much with the act itself but with the hope that inspires it. To the lone heroic figure—Rosa Parks on an Alabama bus, George Patterson facing the Chicago police—we ascribe exceptional moral fortitude. But how do we explain mass protest?

"Social energy is an elusive phenomenon, difficult either to isolate or describe," writes Lawrence Goodwyn, the eloquent chronicler of the Populist movement. In 1883, the Farmers Alliance was an obscure cooperative society in central Texas. In less than a decade it commanded the allegiance of millions of farmers; a few years later it was an empty shell. It is impossible to know with certainty how masses of people acquire the belief that they can alter their fate and why they abandon it. At the heart of every mass movement is a kernel of faith which resists analysis.

This does not mean that the course of social protest is patternless. On the contrary, the history sketched in *This Mighty Dream* reveals certain recurring patterns, which reflect our distinctive national history as well as the universal features of social movements in democratic societies. Knowing how these dilemmas were resolved helps us understand the outcome of past struggles and forecast the challenges which movements of the future will face.

## Constituencies and Change

"What you need here is a union," the Socialist politician Norman Thomas told his young acolytes in Eastern Arkansas. He saw the potential for advancing his principles not only in the Party but in a mass organization of sharecroppers resisting exploitation "at the point of production."

Like the Southern Tenant Farmers Union, the most compelling American movements have combined a response to the immediate issues of a specific social class with a broader vision of change. The IWW grew out of a meeting of radical ideologists who believed in class war and trade unionists who had lived it. The civil rights movement wedded a non-violent direct action philosophy, developed by religious intellectuals, to the indigenous culture and institutions of the black South.

The synthesis is critical. Few Americans become political activists because they envision a new society; most act from self-interest. A social vision which does not address the grievances of particular people has no political constituency and, therefore, little chance of fulfillment. On the other hand, a constituency without a vision of change is no more than an interest group.

Thus, social movements experience an inevitable tension between the pursuit of immediate benefits for a well-defined constituency and a commitment to more fundamental reforms. It is visible in the conflict between the Knights of Labor and the AFL, between the IWW and the craft unionists, between the Amalgamated under "Grandmother" Tighe and the rank-and-file activists of SWOC. After the "crisis of victory" in the mid-1960s, the same tension divided activists who sought to consolidate and extend the position of blacks within the political system and those who challenged the system's legitimacy.

There is a tendency to characterize the more visionary organizations as the more "radical," but the assumption is too simplistic. The "cooperative commonwealth" and "one union for all workers" envisioned by the Knights of Labor were more idealistic aspirations than the "pure and simple unionism" of the AFL. But the Knights were often less militant in defending the concrete interests of their members and their appeal lacked the clarity and immediacy of the AFL's. Intent on establishing a new order between labor and capital, Terence Powderly and other national leaders sometimes lost sight of the grim realities of the existing order and the desperation of their constituents. Their excess of idealism was as great a liability to the union movement as the AFL's selfish realism.

Balancing vision and constituency, realism and idealism, is a universal problem for social movements, whether they are reactionary, reformist, or revolutionary; American, European, or non-Western. But the problem takes a distinctive form in the United States because of the unique features of our social structure and political culture. The natural constituency for social change has lacked a fixed class identity and has always been fractured along ethnic, racial, occupational, and regional lines. As a result, movements have been torn between the political advantages of a broad base and the difficulty of maintaining internal consensus within a divided constituency. Some have foundered on this conflict.

1

The Populists offer perhaps the most poignant example. They recognized that they could not win political power without breaking down the partisan loyalties which divided white Southern farmers from Western farmers and blacks. To a remarkable degree they succeeded. But it was not enough to win, in part because they were unable to capture another key constituency—urban workers. As the opposition counterattacked with crude racial and sectional appeals, the Party's constituents reverted to their traditional loyalties and the movement disintegrated.

The AFL, which emerged at the same time that the Farmers Alliance flourished, took the opposite course. Forswearing political power, it focused its organizing efforts on skilled, native-born workers—those with the strongest bargaining position in the workplace. This strategy worked reasonably well at first in unmechanized, decentralized trades. But in the mass production industries, the AFL's reluctance to organize the unskilled and the foreign-born was self-destructive.

With racial and ethnic movements, divisions have often been manifested along economic lines. The ascendancy of middle-class Chicanos in the Community Service Organization undermined the advocacy stance of the organization and stifled its recruitment among the poor. Within the black movement, class differences, long obscured by the common objective of eliminating segregation, emerged in full force after the civil rights victories of the mid-1960s. What should come next—a black people's movement, a poor people's movement, or an attempt to combine both? After two decades, the debate is still unresolved.

From those who opted for poor people's organizing came the main-

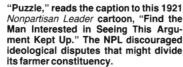

2

"Puzzle," reads the caption to this 1921 *Nonpartisan Leader* cartoon, "Find the Man Interested in Seeing This Argument Kept Up." The NPL discouraged ideological disputes that might divide its farmer constituency.

3

IWW women rally in Massachusetts to protest the trial of two Wobbly organizers.

line of contemporary community protest, broadened to encompass a "majority constituency." These organizations boast a more diverse membership than any protest movement since the CIO, but their social breadth exacted a price. It limited community organizations to a circumscribed range of goals and tactics which were acceptable to all its constituents, a lowest common denominator of protest. That posture is difficult to maintain, and community organizations have tended to drift towards one or another segment of their constituencies or to oscillate between them, never really mobilizing the whole.

The "visions" of American protest movements have also been diverse. They have accommodated an extraordinary range of views and influences—Jeffersonian republicanism, cooperative self-help, libertarian sentiment, Marxian socialism—without, for the most part, feeling the need to choose among them. They have adopted ideas about social change without demanding a consistent and comprehensive critique of American society.

This eclectic approach has been a source of both strength and weakness. It allowed John L. Lewis to hire Communists to organize Catholic workers. It allowed North Dakota farmers to adopt a socialist platform without converting to Socialism. It allowed black nationalists and integrationists to work together, though sometimes uneasily. And it has allowed organizations to respond freshly to their conditions, to define their goals without dogmatic constraints.

"A people's program is whatever program the people themselves decide," pronounced Saul Alinsky. The remark is slightly disingenuous, but it does capture a basic tenet of community organizing in particular and American protest in general.

It is worth noting, however, that few of the organizations described in *This Mighty Dream* maintained their vitality for more than a decade. Without a consistent ideological perspective it is harder to prevent a heterogenous movement from fracturing into its component parts under stress and conflict, as the Populists fractured after 1896. It is harder to maintain a commitment to a broader vision of social change once initial demands are met, as CIO radicals discovered in the 1940s and '50s. Without an ideology, American movements have lacked a prime material for building an enduring culture of protest.

## Culture

By "culture," we mean those forces which can override individual self-interest. There are many examples: racial and ethnic identity, religious and moral values, patriotism, political beliefs, organizational loyalties. Most often, these forces serve to bolster the legitimacy of the existing order and discourage protest. A customary task of social movements, therefore, is to break down the dominant political culture and build an alternative.

The Populists followed a trail blazed by the Grange and other farmers' groups, but went much farther. Traveling lecturers, the rural press, the picnic rallies, and, most importantly, the shared experience of cooperative enterprise all helped to make the movement a "schoolroom," as Goodwyn calls it, where farmers could reassess their allegiances to section, race, and party. Because the movement created its own cultural apparatus, farmers could see themselves as Alliancemen first rather than Northerners or Southerners, white or black, Republican or Democrat.

The Knights of Labor also built upon a fraternal tradition, rooted in the guilds, to create protective enclaves of "workingman's culture." The lodges and halls of later unions served a similar purpose, as did the organizational trappings of the Wobblies—songbooks, emblems, slogans, hobo slang. As with the farmers, however, it was mainly the experience of struggle itself, the hardships of strikes, the bloody battles with employers and police, which eroded ethnic and occupational rivalries and cemented workers' loyalties to "the idea of a union."

When struggle declined, as it did in the 1920s and again after 1950, the slogans became hollow, the lodge rituals empty, the meetings unattended, the songs unsung; the values of solidarity and sacrifice receded. But they were never entirely extinguished, and now show signs of revival. Organized labor created the most enduring protest culture in the nation's history.

For the civil rights movement, the task was relatively straightforward, because black Americans already possessed a cohesive and autonomous culture, which proved to be well suited to mass protest. The institutional expressions of black culture—the dense network of segregated colleges, women's clubs, newspapers, union locals, and small businesses—provided the organizational infrastructure of the movement. The black church provided many of its leaders and organizers, its music and rhetoric, and much of its resilient spirit. But it would be mistaken to assume that any ethnic culture is easily converted to a protest culture. The black ghettos of the North were not receptive to the Southern movement. And when CSO was founded in the late 1940s, California's Mexican-American communities had no institutional base to support it.

Contemporary community organizations which seek a "majority constituency" face an exceptionally hard task. Their members have little in common beyond a low or moderate income and a general sense of powerlessness. Their goals are extremely varied, their organizational experience diffuse and frequently shallow. "Working class culture," always a problematic concept in the United States, has even less resonance than a generation ago. The individualistic values of contemporary society are a more effective brake on collective action than the steel trust's propaganda ever was. Only a movement of a scope and ardor comparable to industrial unionism could break the hold of these values.

## Scale

The dilemmas that plague protest movements are magnified as their scope becomes more ambitious. A farmers movement like the Nonpartisan League in its early stages, operating in a small agricultural state, benefited from the homogeneity of its constituents and the stark polarization between them and their opponents. It did not have to contend with sectional, racial, or deep political cleavages. But as the League expanded beyond North Dakota and staked positions contrary to prevailing patriotic sentiments, it found itself increasingly vulnerable to attack.

Political authority is sufficiently decentralized in the United States

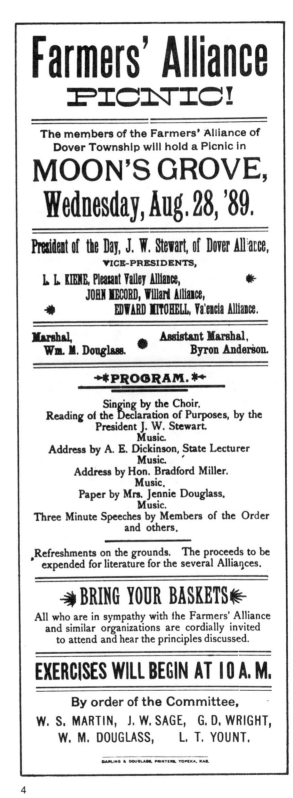

4

to permit local organizations to win significant victories without possessing national power. But localism has its limits. The Birmingham movement could not defeat the city's segregationist establishment without the national prestige of Martin Luther King, Jr. and the intervention of President John F. Kennedy. Even SNCC's Mississippi organizers, militantly localist, eventually sought help from outside the state.

"You've got to attack the problem at its source," stated ACORN leader Charles Crews, and he, like many other protest leaders, concluded that the source is national. For most social change movements in the United States, the issue has not been whether to expand, but how.

One option is replication without centralization; this was the path Alinsky followed in building autonomous neighborhood organizations around the country. It appeals to a strain in our national culture which is deeply suspicious of bureaucratic authority and cherishes direct, participatory democracy. But although Alinsky expected his groups to eventually coalesce and address issues beyond the neighborhood, they have not. Autonomy, once enjoyed, is difficult to surrender.

The black freedom struggle was also decentralized. Local groups operated autonomously, national organizations competed openly for money and publicity, strategies were improvised, often at apparent cross-purposes. But for a crucial five years, between 1960 and 1965, all the competing strains contributed to the momentum of the struggle. As a SNCC activist remarked, "No one really needed 'organization' because we then had a movement."

But a "movement" is impossible to manufacture and difficult to sustain. More often, protest leaders have sought to consolidate their constituencies under a single organizational banner—the People's Party, the Knights of Labor, NWRO, ACORN. This process is sometimes accompanied by bureaucratic centralization which starves grassroots activism. NWRO failed, in part, because its concentration of resources and energies on national welfare reform decimated local chapters. But ACORN's national expansion, which exposed neighborhood activists in the South and West to the protest tactics of the Northeastern cities, may have actually stimulated the militancy of its local affiliates.

Unified mass organization does not create the conflicts between local priorities and national priorities, between democracy and bureaucracy, it simply concentrates them within a single structure. And while scale exacerbates the problems, it does not render them intractable. If social change organizations are sometimes autocratic or sluggish, it is not primarily their size which is to blame but the character and accountability of their organizers and leaders.

## Leadership

The story of Grand Master Workman Terence Powderly and the Knights of Labor is a classic case of unaccountability. Powderly, the chief national spokesman for the union, maintained a very tenuous connection with the rank and file, and his conservative tactical stance was frequently at odds with the more militant locals. This proved disastrous in the national railroad strike of 1886, when the locals refused to honor an unsatisfactory settlement that Powderly had negotiated with the Gould lines.

5

Rev. Adam Clayton Powell addresses a mass meeting in Washington, D.C., in 1942. Powell's charismatic militance was a prototype for civil rights movement leadership.

The rank and file didn't trust his judgment and Powderly did not have sufficient authority to enforce the pact. Employers broke the strike by force and the decline of the Knights commenced.

The story of steel is throughout one of conflict between "top-down" and grassroots leadership. The confict was not only between incompetent craft leaders like "Grandmother" Tighe and the rank and file; even the federated drives to organize the industry in 1919 and in the late 1930s were essentially top-down operations. It is fatuous to assume that the rank and file always knows best; in 1919, for example, when "the dam broke before the district was half worked," the grassroots insistence on a strike may well have been premature. And the rank and file might have lost the battle for recognition in the 1930s without the massive intervention of John L. Lewis and the CIO. But Lewis' autocratic style and his hierarchical approach to organization left an enduring imprint on the Steelworkers' union.

SNCC, CORE, and SCLC were notable for their consensual approach to decision-making, a characteristic shared by many of the local coalitions which were the backbone of the civil rights movement. Leaders exerted influence by dint of persuasion, inspiration, and example rather than hierarchical position. They lacked the power and, for the most part, the inclination to stifle grassroots initiatives and to suppress competing strategies. "King appeared not to direct but to float with the tide of militant direct action," notes historian August Meier, and the same observation applies to many of the more prominent civil rights leaders.

When the tide ran strong, the liabilities of this style were submerged. If organizational structures were too weak to hold leaders accountable, it wasn't noticeable, because the pressure of grassroots activity and intense organizational comeptition kept leaders on course. If the movement emphasized rhetorical power and personal charisma over organizing skills, it hardly mattered, because the rank and file seemed to mobilize itself. Only after 1965, when the movement sought to build a new base in the Northern cities, did these deficiencies become severe handicaps. But by then the mold had set.

It was in reaction to the leadership style of the civil rights movement that community organizers came to appreciate Alinksy's conceptual distinction between the role of the organizer and the role of the leader. The notion of a professional organizer was hardly new. The Populists had their "traveling lecturers," the Nonpartisan League its itinerant recruiters in their model T's paid on commission. The labor unions hired staff by the scores for their big drives. And in civil rights organizations, there were always individuals like Ella Baker and Bob Moses who assumed the unglamorous functions and low profile prescribed by Alinsky.

Community organizing, however, sharpened the definitions of organizational roles, structurally and functionally. Leaders were indigenous, organizers were outsiders; leaders were elected, organizers were hired; leaders addressed the public, organizers operated behind the scenes; leaders set goals, organizers proposed strategies; leaders were accountable to the membership, organizers to the leadership.

This separation of roles is somewhat rigid and artificial. It represents, in part, an adjustment to the increasing reliance of protest organizations on college-educated, middle class staff. But it also reflects a characteristic tendency among community organizers, going back to

**6**

STFU organizers at a meeting of a black local. "Never promise the workers that the Union is going to do something for them," instructed a staff memo. "Let them join the Union and do something themselves. Do not promise to personally lead them out of hard times . . . because you can't do it."

Alinsky, of thinking critically and systematically about organizational structure and accountability. They have devoted much of their craft to de-mystifying leadership, to shaping organizations which would be both decisive and democratic, to reinforcing the principle that it is mass action, not the sentiments of prophets and politicians, that drives the engine of social change.

"I do not want you to follow me or anyone else," Socialist leader and labor organizer Eugene Debs warned his partisans. "If you are looking for a Moses to lead you out of this capitalistic wilderness, you will stay right where you are. I would not lead you into the promised land if I could, because if I could lead you in someone else would lead you out."

## Political Action

The "promised land" for many reformers was the "cooperative commonwealth," an ideal which has always had tremendous resonance in the American protest tradition. From the cooperative stores of the Knights of Labor, to the STFU's Delta Cooperative Farm, to The Woodlawn Organization's experiments in community economic development, social change organizations have sought to create alternative institutions which would be controlled by workers and consumers rather than by capital or government. While some have lasted for decades, none has had the impact its founders envisioned. Still, the cooperative dream has endured as a strategy for social change without coercion or conflict.

By contrast, politics had popularly been viewed as a Faustian bargain, corrupting even those who enter it with the purest motives. But while many organizations at first avoided electoral activity, strategic failures and opportunities often propelled them into the political arena.

When commercial interests crushed the farmer's cooperative crusade in the 1880s, Alliance farmers came to see political power as their trump card and formed the People's Party. However, the Party absorbed opportunists who were willing to sell out the platform to advance their own political and economic interests. The results—internal conflict and electoral defeats—confirmed the farmers' initial fears about political action. The People's Party not only failed, it helped to kill the movement that had spawned it.

Coupled with the failure of other insurgent third-party efforts, the Populists' cautionary tale helps to explain the long anti-electoral tradition in the American labor movement. There were other factors as well. Until the New Deal era, neither major party was especially sympathetic to labor's demands, while the left wing parties were often in disarray or too radical for mainline union leaders. The focus of labor's struggle was the workplace, narrowly defined, and when government intervened in that struggle it was almost always on the wrong side. Unlike the Populists, whose commitment to monetary reform required a legislative solution, labor had little reason to view government as the arbiter of its disputes. It adhered to a notion of "voluntarism," relying on the solidarity of workers, not the sympathies of politicians, to achieve reforms. From the Wobblies to the AFL, so different in most respects, strategists shared the view that political action was a divisive and fruitless sideshow removed from the main arena of struggle with employers.

"Sockless" Jerry Simpson, Populist candidate for Congress at a Harper, Kansas, debate in 1892.

The unions' perspective on electoral activity was radically altered in the 1930s, when the victories of industrial labor were aided and codified by government action. Organized labor remained officially non-partisan, but beginning with Roosevelt's reelection campaign in 1936 it invested heavily in politics, providing campaign foot soldiers and large sums of money to pro-labor candidates.

The civil rights movement also avoided electoral activity for many years. The Republicans, historically the pro-Negro party, were committed to the status quo after 1896; the Democrats were reluctant to alienate their Southern bloc; and political leaders in both parties were openly racist. In the South few blacks could vote and where they could they were generally a small minority, making independent political action unrealistic. But once mass protest secured government protection of the right to vote, movement activists sought to take full advantage of the franchise. Black voters became a potent political force in many localities.

For both the labor and civil rights movements, however, the effect if not the intent of electoral strategies was defensive. They protected the gains which had been won rather than producing new victories.

For disaffected groups, political action is neither an insidious trap nor a panacea. The history of third-party efforts in the U.S. suggests that placing electoral goals ahead of mobilizing and consolidating a mass base is a path to failure. But sometimes, as for the farmers of North Dakota in 1916, choosing politics as a primary strategy is the logical course. Even for movements which don't rely heavily on the ballot box, elections play a crucial role—what Wade Rathke refers to as a "ratifying" function.

Roosevelt's 1936 election victory solidified New Deal support for the unionization of industrial labor. The turnout of 80,000 Mississippi blacks in the "Freedom Vote" campaign demonstrated that voting rights was an urgent issue not just for activists, but for the entire community. The passage of a Lifeline initiative by Little Rock voters ratified ACORN's claim to represent popular disapproval of inequitable utility rates.

But none of these campaigns began with electoral objectives. They began with direct action.

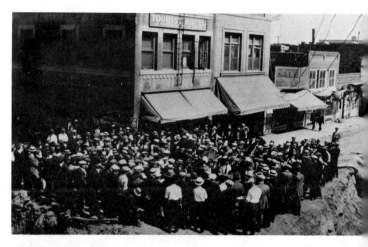

A Wobbly "free speech" action in San Pedro, California. Scores went to jail to challenge the ban on public speaking.

8

## Direct Action

Outward forms of direct action—the phsyical assertion of common purpose—have changed little over the years. The Freedom Riders, provoking arrests with acts of civil disobedience, resemble the Wobblies who filled the Western jails in defense of free speech. Citizen lobbyists, jamming the halls of government to demand lower utility rates, are akin to the North Dakota farmers who stormed the state capitol to hold legislators accountable to campaign promises. The "innovative" tactics of contemporary unions mimic the 19th century practices of the Knights of Labor.

Direct action has consistently served to build internal solidarity. But its external functions have varied; tactics evolved to meet particular circumstances. Rallies and marches were demonstrative; they defined the issues to the community and demonstrated that masses of people were concerned about them. Other actions were reactive: when unemployed

9     At the March on Washington, 1963. National television coverage played a crucial role in civil rights movement strategy.

10     A utility rate protest in the mid-1970s.

families were threatened with eviction, their neighbors stood in front of the door to block the marshalls; when scabs were expected, pickets were posted to keep them out. Finally, there were "offensive" tactics—withholding wheat from the market, boycotts, work stoppages, rent strikes—consciously designed to exert economic pressure on an opponent.

Civil rights movement strategists conceived a new function for direct action. "When you start talking about nonviolent direct action, you're talking about spiritual concepts," observes C.T. Vivian, a founder of the Nashville sit-in movement. "You're not really talking about politics, nor are you talking about economics." The hope was that adversaries confronted by Christian nonviolence would abandon their segregationist policies.

In fact, blacks did not obtain victories by changing the hearts of their oppressors, but by exerting political and economic pressure on them. What was unique was the extent to which that pressure came from converts to the cause outside the affected communities. In the past, union organizers had mobilized public opinion against employers but the primary goal was to disrupt production. Southern blacks had much less capacity to intefere with the essential functions of the economy, and a determined establishment, such as Birmingham's, could ride out the protests. But by using tactics that attracted national media coverage, the movement overcame local intransigence. Nonviolent demonstrations provoked violent reactions, and the images of unresisting blacks being beaten by white mobs and policemen unleashed a flood of moral outrage.

While the Homestead conflicts and the Memorial Day massacre could hardly be described as "media events," it would not be inappropriate to describe the Freedom Rides, the Birmingham and Selma marches in that fashion. It is worth noting, for example, that the Selma campaign was preceded by one of the worst outbreaks of violence in the Movement period, a police riot in Marion, Alabama. But for the national movement, it was a non-event because it wasn't filmed; white townspeople sprayed paint on the lenses of TV cameras, beat up camera crews, and shot out the lights.

There have been few tactical breakthroughs since the 1960s but community organizing has kept direct action very much alive. It borrowed tactics from past movements and adapted them to a different political environment. While the conflicts between blacks and whites, like those between labor and management, were easy to comprehend, the source of the problems in urban neighborhoods was less clear, the power relationships more subtle and diffuse. A new function for direct action was to make hidden conflicts explicit, to "give the issue a face" as some organizers put it. Actions were designed to pin responsibility for the resolution of community issues on specific individuals.

As the "majority constituency" organizations expanded their scope far beyond the neighborhood, targets became increasingly distant and inaccessible. Mounting direct action campaigns on corporate empires or bureaucracies in Washington, D.C. is more problematic than keeping the pressure on the local slumlord or City Hall. For the labor movement, as well, customary tactics are less effective now that production has become less centralized and companies are using more sophisticated union-busting techniques. The traditional forms of direct action are not obsolete, but their strategic application has become somewhat predictable, and opponents have learned how to resist them.

## Resistance

The forces opposed to change have deployed an array of repressive weapons against the challenges posed by social movements. Courts provided injunctions against strikes and demonstrations; banks and merchants cut off credit; empoyers fired activists and landlords evicted them from their farms and homes; police, vigilantes, and private armies bloodied protestors and sometimes murdered them. In tandem with repression came "redbaiting," remarkably durable in a nation which has never been seriously threatened by a Communist insurgency. "Capital as a rule is thoroughly organized against the interest of the laboring class," concluded Populist organizer S.O. Daws. "But when the laboring class begins to organize, they call it Communism and other hard names, which is unjust."

Movements have defended themselves in various ways. One natural reaction is to fight back in kind—to return violence with violence, slander with slander, reprisals with sabotage. Another is to seek protective association with neutral authorities, such as clergy, academics, and elected officials, who can lend legitimacy to an unpopular cause. Some groups use repression itself as a moral issue to mobilize sympathizers and rally the faithful.

None of these defenses has proved entirely reliable. Counterforce is rarely effective in the long run, because the opposition usually has access to more powerful weapons; strikers could beat up scabs, but they were no match for the National Guard. "Legitimators" who associated too long with unpopular groups generally ended up de-legitimated. Moral outrage worked for the civil rights protestors in the early 1960s, but not for the Wobblies during World War I.

One reason the civil rights movement prevailed was its capacity to absorb attack without losing momentum. When the key IWW leaders went to jail, the crusade to free them drained the movement's energies and organizing suffered; when key civil rights leaders went to jail, the mass marches continued, larger than ever. The best defense against repression, in the long run, was to maintain the offense—the course of action that brought a movement closest to the gates of power.

Some opponents came to the same conclusion: a movement without forward momentum would soon collapse. It was easier to co-opt a movement, they reasoned, than to crush it. Democrats adopted this strategy in 1896, when they switched from brutal attacks on Populists to jumping on the silver bandwagon. Mayors used it in the 1970s, when they blunted demands for neighborhood empowerment by incorporating groups into elaborate but powerless "citizen participation" forums.

But co-optation sometimes boomerangs, when it comes too little, too late. The employee representation plans introduced by the steel industry after the NIRA became convenient rostrums for protest leaders rather than pliant company unions. The Kennedy Administration's attempt to direct black activism into voting rights ultimately heightened racial conflict rather than defusing it. Even a token concession, exploited skillfully, can sustain the momentum of a protest campaign.

From the perspective of the opposition, then, the ideal response to protest is no response, the ideal form of resistance is invisible resistance. If those who might benefit from change are fragmented into competing

11

interest groups, they represent little threat to the status quo. If the "great social questions" are deemed irrelevant, the people who raise them can be dismissed.

With only slight exaggeration, this is where we stand today. It is no wonder that many of those committed to change are pessimistic. For no matter how adept we are at resolving the dilemmas of mass action, we—like the activists of the past—are constrained by the realities of culture and power in our nation. And those realities seem more resistant to change than they have in many decades.

Yet it is dangerous, as well as arrogant, to prejudge the nature of one's time and a society's potential for change. What realist in 1883 could have foreseen a movement of millions in a dispirited fraternity of Texas farmers? What realist in the prosperous and complacent '20s could have anticipated the depth of collapse in the American economy and the lightning triumph of industrial unionism? What realist contemplating the gulf between the "silent majority" and the invisible poor in the Eisenhower era could have imagined an ACORN?

"All those early sit-inners and SNCC people . . . really believed they were going to win," recalls a movement veteran. "They really sort of thought there was an end in sight." And they were vindicated, as brave and resourceful dreamers are repeatedly vindicated, not just in the folklore of the faithful but in the unsentimental eye of history.

12

Textile workers on strike in Lawrence, Massachusetts, face the state militia, 1912.

13